An Analysis of

Michel Foucault's

Discipline and Punish

Meghan Kallman
with
Rachele Dini

Published by Macat International Ltd
24:13 Coda Centre, 189 Munster Road, London SW6 6AW.

Distributed exclusively by Routledge
2 Park Square, Milton Park, Abingdon, Oxon OX14 4RN
711 Third Avenue, New York, NY 10017, USA

Routledge is an imprint of the Taylor & Francis Group, an informa business

www.macat.com
info@macat.com

Cataloguing in Publication Data
A catalogue record for this book is available from the British Library.
Library of Congress Cataloguing-in-Publication Data is available upon request.
Cover illustration: Etienne Gilfillan

ISBN 978-1-912303-75-5 (hardback)
ISBN 978-1-912127-51-1 (paperback)
ISBN 978-1-912282-63-0 (e-book)

Notice
The information in this book is designed to orientate readers of the work under analysis,
to elucidate and contextualise its key ideas and themes, and to aid in the development
of critical thinking skills. It is not meant to be used, nor should it be used, as a
substitute for original thinking or in place of original writing or research. References and
notes are provided for informational purposes and their presence does not constitute
endorsement of the information or opinions therein. This book is presented solely for
educational purposes. It is sold on the understanding that the publisher is not engaged
to provide any scholarly advice. The publisher has made every effort to ensure that
this book is accurate and up-to-date, but makes no warranties or representations with
regard to the completeness or reliability of the information it contains. The information
and the opinions provided herein are not guaranteed or warranted to produce particular
results and may not be suitable for students of every ability. The publisher shall not be
liable for any loss, damage or disruption arising from any errors or omissions, or from
the use of this book, including, but not limited to, special, incidental, consequential or
other damages caused, or alleged to have been caused, directly or indirectly, by the
information contained within.

CONTENTS

THE MACAT LIBRARY

The Macat Library is a series of unique academic explorations of seminal works in the humanities and social sciences – books and papers that have had a significant and widely recognised impact on their disciplines. It has been created to serve as much more than just a summary of what lies between the covers of a great book. It illuminates and explores the influences on, ideas of, and impact of that book. Our goal is to offer a learning resource that encourages critical thinking and fosters a better, deeper understanding of important ideas.

Each publication is divided into three Sections: Influences, Ideas, and Impact. Each Section has four Modules. These explore every important facet of the work, and the responses to it.

This Section-Module structure makes a Macat Library book easy to use, but it has another important feature. Because each Macat book is written to the same format, it is possible (and encouraged!) to cross-reference multiple Macat books along the same lines of inquiry or research. This allows the reader to open up interesting interdisciplinary pathways.

To further aid your reading, lists of glossary terms and people mentioned are included at the end of this book (these are indicated by an asterisk [*] throughout) – as well as a list of works cited.

Macat has worked with the University of Cambridge to identify the elements of critical thinking and understand the ways in which six different skills combine to enable effective thinking.
Three allow us to fully understand a problem; three more give us the tools to solve it. Together, these six skills make up the **PACIER** model of critical thinking. They are:

ANALYSIS – understanding how an argument is built
EVALUATION – exploring the strengths and weaknesses of an argument
INTERPRETATION – understanding issues of meaning

CREATIVE THINKING – coming up with new ideas and fresh connections
PROBLEM-SOLVING – producing strong solutions
REASONING – creating strong arguments

To find out more, visit **WWW.MACAT.COM.**

CRITICAL THINKING AND *DISCIPLINE AND PUNISH*

Primary critical thinking skill: ANALYSIS
Secondary critical thinking skill: REASONING

Michel Foucault is famous as one of the 20th-century's most innovative thinkers – and his work on *Discipline and Punish* was so original and offered models so useful to other scholars that the book now ranks among the most influential academic works ever published.

Foucault's aim is to trace the way in which incarceration was transformed between the seventeenth and twentieth centuries. What started as a spectacle, in which ritual punishments were focused on the prisoner's body, eventually became a matter of the private disciplining of a delinquent soul.

Foucault's work is renowned for its original insights, and *Discipline and Punish* contains several of his most compelling observations. Much of the focus of the book is on making new connections between knowledge and power, leading Foucault to sketch out a new interpretation of the relationship between *voir, savoir* and *pouvoir* – or, 'to see is to know is to have power.' Foucault also dwells in fascinating detail on the true implications of a uniquely creative solution to the problems generated by incarcerating large numbers of criminals in a confined space – Jeremy Bentham's 'panopticon,' a prison constructed around a central tower from which hidden guards might – or might not – be monitoring any given prisoner at any given time. As Foucualt points out, the panopticon creates a prison in which inmates will discipline themselves, for fear of punishment, even when there are no guards present. He goes on to apply this insight to the manner in which all of us behave in the outside world – a world in which CCTV and speed cameras are explicitly designed to modify our behavior.

Foucault's highly original vision of prisons also ties them to broader structures of power, allowing him to argue that all previous conceptions of prison are misleading, even wrong. For Foucault, the ultimate purpose of incarceration is neither to punish inmates, nor to reduce crime. It is to produce delinquency as a way of enabling the state to control and of structure crime.

ABOUT THE AUTHOR OF THE ORIGINAL WORK

Michel Foucault was born in 1926 into a wealthy and conservative French family. He studied philosophy, but being gay in a homophobic society took its toll and after a suicide attempt in his early 20s, he was treated in a psychiatric hospital. Foucault is considered one of the most important modern thinkers. His analyses of the interplay of power, knowledge, and the makeup of the individual are considered key contributions to a wide range of academic fields, including sociology, history, and philosophy. Foucault died in 1984 at the age of 57.

ABOUT THE AUTHORS OF THE ANALYSIS

Dr Meghan Kallman is a Postdoctoral Research Fellow at Brown University, working in the Department of Sociology. Her research focuses on bureaucratized morality and public altruism. In her spare time, she plays accordion in the Extraordinary Rendition Band, a guerilla activist collective in Providence, RI.

Dr Rachele Dini studied at Cambridge, King's College London and University College London. Much of her current work focuses on the representation of production and consumption in modern and contemporary Anglo-American fiction. She has taught at Cambridge and for the Foundation for International Education, and is now Ledturer in English at the University of Roehampton. Her first monograph, *Consumerism, Waste and Re-use in Twentieth-century Fiction: Legacies of the Avant-Garde*, was published by Palgrave Macmillan in 2016.

ABOUT MACAT

GREAT WORKS FOR CRITICAL THINKING

Macat is focused on making the ideas of the world's great thinkers accessible and comprehensible to everybody, everywhere, in ways that promote the development of enhanced critical thinking skills.

It works with leading academics from the world's top universities to produce new analyses that focus on the ideas and the impact of the most influential works ever written across a wide variety of academic disciplines. Each of the works that sit at the heart of its growing library is an enduring example of great thinking. But by setting them in context – and looking at the influences that shaped their authors, as well as the responses they provoked – Macat encourages readers to look at these classics and game-changers with fresh eyes. Readers learn to think, engage and challenge their ideas, rather than simply accepting them.

'Macat offers an amazing first-of-its-kind tool for interdisciplinary learning and research. Its focus on works that transformed their disciplines and its rigorous approach, drawing on the world's leading experts and educational institutions, opens up a world-class education to anyone.'

Andreas Schleicher
Director for Education and Skills, Organisation for Economic Co-operation and Development

'Macat is taking on some of the major challenges in university education … They have drawn together a strong team of active academics who are producing teaching materials that are novel in the breadth of their approach.'

Prof Lord Broers,
former Vice-Chancellor of the University of Cambridge

'The Macat vision is exceptionally exciting. It focuses upon new modes of learning which analyse and explain seminal texts which have profoundly influenced world thinking and so social and economic development. It promotes the kind of critical thinking which is essential for any society and economy. This is the learning of the future.'

Rt Hon Charles Clarke, former UK Secretary of State for Education

'The Macat analyses provide immediate access to the critical conversation surrounding the books that have shaped their respective discipline, which will make them an invaluable resource to all of those, students and teachers, working in the field.'

Professor William Tronzo, University of California at San Diego

WAYS IN TO THE TEXT

KEY POINTS

- Michel Foucault (1926–84) was a French social philosopher and historian.

- *Discipline and Punish* proposes a theory of modern power relations—the power held by different sections of society— by tracing a history of the modern prison and its impact on other social institutions such as hospitals, factories, schools, and workplaces.

- *Discipline and Punish* has had an impact on the approach taken by scholars in the humanities and social sciences in understanding power, through its investigation of the roles of surveillance*—systematic monitoring—and knowledge-creation in constructing both individuals and relationships.

Who Was Michel Foucault?

Michel Foucault, the author of *Discipline and Punish: The Birth of the Prison* (1975), was a radical French social philosopher, historian, and literary critic. Today, he is widely recognized as being one of the most influential contemporary thinkers in both the social sciences and the humanities.

The son of a surgeon, Foucault grew up in a wealthy and socially conservative home in western France, and enjoyed a privileged education. Against his father's wishes, he studied philosophy* and the history of science at university, and wrote his PhD thesis on the history of madness. In it, he drew a distinction between mental illness and madness; the latter, he argued, is a social construct based on subjective assumptions.

The thesis was published in English as *Madness and Civilization* and later as *History of Madness*. It was extremely well received, winning the prestigious Medal of the Centre national de la recherche scientifique (the French National Center for Scientific Research), the main governmental research organization in France. Foucault's next books were *The Birth of the Clinic* (1963), *The Order of Things* (1966), and *The Archaeology of Knowledge* (1969).

Throughout his life, Foucault remained committed to left-wing politics: he was, for example, a leading anti-prison activist. Much French left-wing activism in the 1960s and 1970s was dominated by certain Marxist* ideas—that is, beliefs derived from the work of the German political theorist Karl Marx*—about the need to end structures of power that exploited wage earners and others. Foucault's intellectual contributions, however, were based on his claim that no one person or group alone possesses power: as the individual is constructed from the power relations in which he or she lives, escape from those power relations is impossible.

What Does *Discipline and Punish* Say?

In *Discipline and Punish*, Foucault departs from the idea of power as something exerted by the government, by a king, or by those with material wealth. Power, he says, is "discipline."* It is important to note the particular way in which Foucault uses the word, however; for him, discipline is not the top-down application of direct coercion* but power used in a way that makes the individual self-regulate.

Taking the penal system as an example, he demonstrates how the discipline of the prison is a specific form of power that has become embedded in society since its emergence in the seventeenth century. It is, in other words, "historically contingent,"* meaning it grew out of a particular historical context.

Beyond the history of such disciplinary procedures, Foucault is concerned with the techniques and mechanisms of power that use these approaches. In this work, Foucault begins a deep examination of the relationship between the physical body, the individual, and what he calls "power-knowledge"*[1]— the marriage of power and knowledge that allows the powerful to classify and control people and things. These are all themes that appear throughout his writings.

Discipline and Punish argues that social institutions exercise power and discipline on the bodies and souls of their subjects through *le regard**—the "gaze."[2] Forming this argument, he turns to a discussion of the Panopticon,* a model for a prison invented by the British social reformer Jeremy Bentham* in the late eighteenth century. The Panopticon was designed so that the inmates cannot see their guards and, therefore, never know if they are being watched or not; it is the perpetual possibility of observation that encourages them to behave. Foucault suggests that the Panopticon and the mechanisms of power it contains extend beyond the prison and into other institutions of society (a driver who cannot be certain that she or he is not being tracked by a speed camera, for example, may choose not to speed "just in case"). According to this view, behavior is conditioned by the awareness of the possibility of control.

For Foucault, the individual is essentially a product of this monitoring and control. Surveillance —systematic monitoring—by government institutions produces "docile bodies,"[3] which Foucault defines as bodies that can be monitored and psychologically controlled, and which are then trained to self-govern. Put simply, we are the sum of what we abstain from doing for fear of being seen, judged, or punished.

Why Does *Discipline and Punish* Matter?

Discipline and Punish is considered one of the modern classics of sociological, historical, and philosophical thought. The groundbreaking analysis of power that Foucault presents in his study of social institutions has produced important insights into how individuals and masses are governed. It traces the evolution of modern power structures—such as current prison systems—and considers their effects on human freedom and identity. *Discipline and Punish* is also unique in its approach to its argument: it is not so much a theory of power as a history of its transformation. Foucault's historical approach was designed to allow for the study of different institutions and power structures; the work itself was not intended as a critique of any one specific system, but was, rather, a way to understand how power itself works.

Foucault's analyses encouraged scholars to dramatically re-evaluate how they view the operation of power, knowledge, and what constitutes the individual. Even though some sociologists may not agree with Foucault's understanding of power, there are few trained sociologists who are unfamiliar with it.

Discipline and Punish has had an impact on other disciplines as well. Foucault's recognition that individuals are shaped by the systems of power and knowledge they inhabit has been widely applied in academic debates about human agency and choice and in discussions about identity. The Foucauldian understanding of power and concepts such as discourse* (for Foucault, a way of speaking arising from the influence of history and power—but a term often used for the exchange of ideas, and the way that this exchange defines how something is understood), "power-knowledge,"[4] and panopticism* (the theory that the Panopticon prison is a model for all power relations in society), for example, have not only become part of the vocabulary of sociology,* but appear in disciplines as diverse as history,* economics,* anthropology,* and political science.*

Scholars in fields as varied as cultural studies*, media studies,* and literary studies* have applied Foucault's ideas to the analysis of power relations in literature, music, film, and television. The theory advanced in *Discipline and Punish* is often used to understand how individuals internalize power, and the effect this has on both social relations and the possibility of resistance.

Foucault's ideas have gained new relevance in current debates on individual privacy in the digital age. His identification of the practical benefits of surveillance for social institutions, as well as its human toll, anticipated many of the discussions we have today about the effects of living under the gaze of closed circuit TV (CCTV)* cameras. Similarly, the disclosures made in 2013 by the whistle-blower Edward Snowden,* revealing the extent of the surveillance of US citizens conducted by the state agency known as the National Security Agency (NSA),* in many ways confirm aspects of Foucault's thesis.

NOTES

1   Michel Foucault, *Discipline and Punish*: *The Birth of the Prison* (Sheridan, NY: Vintage Books, 1979), 27.

2   Foucault, *Discipline and Punish*, 96.

3   Foucault, *Discipline and Punish*, 135.

4   Foucault, *Discipline and Punish*, 27.

SECTION 1
INFLUENCES

THE AUTHOR AND THE HISTORICAL CONTEXT

KEY POINTS

- Michel Foucault's text, with its novel ideas about power, has been a key work for a range of academic disciplines. It continues to be relevant, as new concerns arise about such issues as state surveillance* of public areas and the Internet.

- Foucault's ideas were shaped by his early experiences, especially his repressive upbringing (being gay), his personal experiences of the French psychiatric system, and his involvement with prison reform groups.

- Foucault's beliefs were also formed by his involvement in radical left-wing French politics and the students' riots of 1968, which had a deep effect on French thought and society.

Why Read This Text?

Michel Foucault's *Discipline and Punish: The Birth of the Prison* (1975) is a key text for a number of different disciplines, including sociology* (the study of the history and structure of societies), philosophy* (the study of fundamental human problems related to reality, knowledge and existence), and history.* It offers a unique analysis of the evolution of power and modern power structures. In doing so, it asks its readers to rethink taken-for-granted ideas about the nature of power, reason, and the formation of the individual.

Historians are still reading *Discipline and Punish* because of Foucault's claims about history. Criminologists (scholars of matters relating to crime and criminal behavior) are still reading the text

> ❝ I'm not making a problem out of a personal question; I make of a personal question an absence of a problem. ❞
> Michel Foucault, *The Chomsky–Foucault Debate*

because of Foucault's theories about the development and workings of modern prisons. Philosophers are still reading the text because of what it says about the nature of reason and rationality.* And scholars interested in power, from various fields and disciplines, are still reading the text because of the radically new way it looked at the nature of modern power. Given the long-lasting questions about power, the nature of reason, the role of punishment in society, and the forms in which punishment takes, it is unlikely that *Discipline and Punish* will lose its relevancy in the near future. Concerns about the use and abuse of surveillance techniques, such as the explosion of video cameras monitoring public places and cyberveillance* (monitoring of Internet use), has given the text new relevance.

Author's Life
Michel Foucault (1926–84) grew up in a wealthy, socially conservative family in France. Foucault's father was a surgeon, and pushed his son to follow in his footsteps. Foucault resisted, and instead went to the Lycée Henri-IV, an elite public high school in Paris, where he studied philosophy under Jean Hyppolite*—an expert on the nineteenth-century philosopher Hegel.* In 1946, Foucault entered the École normale supérieure (ENS) in Paris, the most prestigious humanities university in France, where he studied under the influential Marxist* philosopher Louis Althusser.* He received a degree in psychology in 1948 and a second degree in philosophy in 1951, working with the equally influential philosopher Maurice Merleau-Ponty,* noted for his work in the field of phenomenology*—roughly, a philosophical

approach that emphasizes the nature and role of perception in the formation of consciousness.

Foucault admitted throughout his career that his life story had a strong influence on the books he wrote: notably his sexuality and his personal experiences with madness and prison systems. Foucault was gay and his early career was framed by the repression of his sexual identity. In 1948, he attempted suicide and received psychiatric treatment in Paris. Doctors diagnosed later suicide attempts as his reaction to the social shame attached to being openly gay in a society that saw homosexuality as a curse.

Foucault's concern with power, madness, and sexuality turns up again and again in his writings. His first book, *Madness and Civilization* (1961), dealt with psychiatry,* a practice with which he had been closely involved both as a patient and later, in the 1950s, as a researcher in a psychiatric hospital. Both psychology* and phenomenology, the subjects of his first two university degrees, are ever-present in the theory and approach of his books. Moreover, his social identity and concern about oppression can be seen throughout his work.

Foucault's political involvement increased in the early 1970s, when he helped found the Prison Information Group, which attempted to focus the attention of the press and the public on prison conditions. We must thank this period of political activism and Foucault's writing on disciplinary institutions for the eventual production of *Discipline and Punish*.

Author's Background

Foucault wrote *Discipline and Punish* at a time of intense sociocultural and political upheaval. France in the 1960s saw a number of conflicts. These included opposition to the country's role in the Vietnam War* (a war fought in Laos, Cambodia, and Vietnam between 1955 and 1975, in which the US engaged North Vietnamese forces sponsored by the communist states of the Soviet Union and China), its treatment of its colonies (and the colonial* system itself), and the structure of its education system. Critics attacked the latter for placing the children of the rich in schools that prepared them for the best jobs. There were also deep anti-capitalist feelings, which gave rise to strikes and occupations of university buildings and factories across the country.

This unrest peaked with the Paris Riots of 1968,* which saw university students occupy the Sorbonne, one of Europe's most distinguished universities, to protest against the capitalist system and "traditional" values, and a two-week general strike involving 11 million workers during which the French economy basically ground to a halt. The government itself stopped functioning when the country's president secretly fled for a few hours. This period had a deep impact on French society, and was viewed as a watershed moment.

This context provides an important key to understanding the origins of Foucault's work: as well as being a scholar, Foucault was active in various left-wing movements. He was involved in anti-colonialist efforts, including supporting the Algerian war* for independence from French rule (1954–62), and in the anti-psychiatry movement* of the 1960s, which opposed practices such as electroshock treatment and lobotomy (a now discredited treatment for mental illness that involved partly destroying the frontal lobes of the brain). He also supported the Iranian Revolution* of 1978, writing articles for the Italian newspaper *Corriere della Sera* and for the French news magazine *Le Nouvel Observateur*. His interest, however, was in the power dynamics playing out rather than in the political interests of any one party. Foucault's concern with the revolution was with its capacity to undermine and then remove the previous Iranian government and power, rather than with the system that would replace the country's monarchy.

Foucault's critiques of colonial oppression, totalitarianism* (a system of government in which the citizen is fully subject to the power of the state), and psychiatry go hand in hand with his views on sexual repression and the "power-knowledge"* complex—the way those in power control information or knowledge. If, on the surface, *Discipline and Punish* is a history of the modern prison and modern methods of punishment, it is also a critique of modern society's ability to encourage or force individuals into self-regulation and conformity.

MODULE 2
ACADEMIC CONTEXT

KEY POINTS

- Foucault came of age at a time when left-wing thought was dominated by the philosophical approaches known as existentialism* and phenomenology,* and the economic and social analytical methods of Marxism.* Challenging those ideas, he moved close to "poststructuralist"* thought with his arguments that human identity is socially and historically constructed.

- Foucault attacked the leading French philosopher Jean-Paul Sartre,* criticizing him for focusing too much on the individual, and not enough on the wider system that molds the individual.

- Influenced by the German philosopher Friedrich Nietzsche,* Foucault believed that rationality,* punishment, and power are not fixed ideas, but rather, they develop out of the history of any particular society.

The Work in its Context

Michel Foucault described his book *Discipline and Punish* as a "history of the modern soul."[1] The work marked a sharp departure from both the Marxism that dominated left-wing political thought at the time and structuralism* (the position that the analysis of human experience and culture requires the identification of ideological, sociocultural, and economic structures underlying them). The key philosophical movements during Foucault's youth were existentialism (a philosophical approach that emphasizes the experience and nature of the human individual), phenomenology (a study that focuses on the

> **❝ The 'Enlightenment', which discovered the liberties, also invented the disciplines. ❞**
>
> Michel Foucault, *Discipline and Punish: The Birth of the Prison*

nature and role of perception in the formation of consciousness), and Marxism (an understanding of social and political processes founded, very roughly, on a critical analysis of capitalism). These three movements were united by their "humanist"* core, especially the belief that action is determined by human nature, and class or social inequality, rather than by God.

In the 1950s and 1960s, these approaches were challenged by structuralism, a theory that says human activity and thought are socially constructed through language. Structuralists believe that the meaning we give to particular events, moments, people, and activities is entirely based on our belief system, historical context, cultural background, and language. Foucault built on this idea, but took it further. He associated himself with poststructuralism* by claiming that individual identity and meaning are not fixed, but are subject to interpretation depending on one's circumstance and perspective (the position from which you are viewing things).

Poststructuralists would argue that texts can be understood in the same way. Their meaning is contingent* on—that is, it depends on—circumstance, perspective, and time. A book, a political speech, or another text might be interpreted in many different ways, and these interpretations are entirely contingent upon the reader. In this approach, Foucault would argue that knowledge and identity are socially constructed: they are not natural, being the product of social norms, belief, or customs. This understanding can then be extended to the prison system, which, similarly, is not a basic, fixed part of society, but a practice that is changeable.

Overview of the Field

The philosophers who contributed the most to the schools of thought identified above were the philosophers Maurice Merleau-Ponty* and Jean-Paul Sartre. These thinkers did not so much influence Foucault directly as shape the fields in which he worked, and create ideas that Foucault ended up rejecting. Along with the phenomenologist Merleau-Ponty, Foucault was concerned with individual, subjective, and bodily experience, and emphasized the importance of this type of experience in understanding the political and social world. Merleau-Ponty's philosophy approached the universal human condition through the body and the way the body sees and feels the world, and the order and meaning it gives to what it perceives. Foucault, however, rejected the idea of a universal human experience of the world.

Sartre's work provides an important context to Foucault's intellectual growth and philosophical approach. Both Sartre and Foucault sympathized with marginalized groups, such as ethnic minorities, homosexuals, and prisoners. These feelings inspired them to political activism. Foucault distanced himself, however, from Sartre's philosophical work, and often argued against Sartre's views. Although they shared some ideas, it is useful to see their projects as separate, even in opposition. Foucault criticized Sartre's emphasis of the individual experience, terming it "transcendental narcissism." By this, Foucault meant that Sartre placed too much importance on the individual subject and too little importance on the system(s) in which individuals find themselves. The "transcendental narcissism" insult was an attack on the way Sartre put the individual at the center of the system, as opposed to accepting that the individual is constructed by the system.

By rejecting the idea of a universal human nature, Foucault was seen as close to structuralism and poststructuralism. Structuralism shares similar concerns to Foucault's—namely, how individuals develop their identities through language. And poststructuralism's idea that entities such as a text or an action can have a variety of interpretations is close to Foucault's understanding of the way knowledge and knowledge systems can be shaped and pushed in different directions.

Academic Influences

Although Foucault's academic influences were many and varied, it can certainly be said that structuralism, poststructuralism, and the work of the nineteenth-century German philosopher Friedrich Nietzsche had a big impact on him.

Foucault's analysis of the development of the prison as a product of wider structural and historical forces suggests the influence of structuralist thinking. The structuralist approach sees individual people as molded by their institutions (school, for example, or the legal system). Foucault did not take the institution of the prison or the individual as a given but, rather, focused on how they were created. The influence of poststructuralism can also be seen in Foucault's claim, throughout *Discipline and Punish*, that the penal system has multiple meanings: it can be both a good and a repressive force.

Foucault, however, rejected his placement within these schools of thought. He insisted that the text's use of a method he called "genealogy"* was its main contribution. It is here that Nietzsche's influence is clear, particularly his studies of morality. Foucault's project on the "genealogy of knowledge"[2] is a direct reference to Nietzsche's concept of a "genealogy of morals."[3] Nietzsche did not take morality as a given, but tried, rather, to account for the ways in which the historical context shapes the values and morals that we have.

This approach influenced the claim Foucault makes in *Discipline and Punish* that our ideas about rationality, punishment, and power inherited from the Enlightenment* (the period of European intellectual history, roughly 1650 to 1780, in which rational thought and behavior were emphasized over religion and superstition) are similarly historically contingent and that one can trace their evolution.

Genealogy can be understood as a style of inquiry that attempts to explain the present by looking to the past; it attempts to trace how we got from "there" to "here." For Foucault, it was genealogy that produced his insights about the nature of discipline* and power, and how they served to construct the self.

NOTES

1   Michel Foucault, *Discipline and Punish*: *The Birth of the Prison* (Sheridan, NY: Vintage Books, 1979), 23.

2   Foucault, *Discipline and Punish*, 27.

3   Friedrich Wilhelm Nietzsche, *The Genealogy of Morals* (London and New York: Macmillan, 1897).

THE PROBLEM

KEY POINTS

- Foucault's work explores how the norms of proper behavior, rationality, and the exercise of power are based on the historical context, and change over time.

- His approach angered many other philosophers, who felt that the aim of their discipline was to search for universal truths.

- Foucault tries to show that power in society has evolved to control and punish "bad" behavior in more subtle and widespread ways than in the past. However, he rejects the common idea that we have been steadily marching toward a more rational system.

Core Question

In *Discipline and Punish*, Michel Foucault sought to understand how the modern individual came to be and how modern forms of power differed from older forms. His project was not merely a description of a certain modern type of power but was, rather, an explanation of how that form of power came to be.

Foucault did this by focusing on the changing relationship between the human body and power; this changing relationship, he argued, effected the operations of power in general. Whereas the body used to be something to be punished corporally, by means of public torture or even death, now the body is something acted upon by way of norms, corrections, and regulations. Foucault was concerned with the ways in which the individual became the target and the product of power. This occurs through the communication of norms for behavior,

> ❝ There is no power relation without the correlative constitution of a field of knowledge, nor any knowledge that does not presuppose and constitute at the same time power relations. ❞
>
> Michel Foucault, *Discipline and Punish: The Birth of the Prison*

which the individual is supposed to accept.

Through this, Foucault wanted to show that there is a relationship between power and knowledge. Institutional power—the power of the schools and the justice system, for example—and the construction of knowledge are deeply connected, and, according to Foucault, together they shape individuals' desires and the way they understand their place in the world. Every social norm, every impulse that society takes for granted, Foucault sought to show, is historically produced and contingent upon the systems of knowledge that created it. Power rests in the production of what is "normal." Individuals want to be "normal," and so they act in accordance with these norms.

The Participants

While other scholars studied institutions or social structures, Foucault termed himself a historian of systems of thought. He took as his unit of analysis the language that shapes social reality—in essence, he attempts to understand the language and thinking that create different systems of thought. This was a novel approach to understanding history, leading him into largely uncharted territory.

Foucault angered many philosophers with this approach, since the main concern of philosophy is generally considered to be with universal truths—that is, with the study of knowledge that is valid in all times and places. In this sense, philosophy* is understood to be independent of history and culture. Foucault argued against this by placing language and thought in particular social, cultural, and historical contexts, and his strongest critics were those who objected to these premises.

Among his best-known critics was the German sociologist Jürgen Habermas.* Foucault also faced intense objections from Marxist* philosophers who approached power from a materialist* point of view—that is, they saw power as the result of social inequality and the uneven distribution of wealth. These critics included the thinkers Simone de Beauvoir,* noted for her contribution to feminist* theory, and the existentialist* Jean-Paul Sartre,* who had viewed Foucault's previous work *The Order of Things* (1966) as a right-wing attack on Marxism and its related fields. These included phenomenology* (an approach to philosophy that centers on the nature and role of perception in consciousness) and existentialism,[1] a philosophical approach established on the principle that the individual is the foundation of meaning.

The Contemporary Debate

Following in the footsteps of his former teacher, the philosopher Jean Hyppolite,* Foucault rejected the classic interpretation of reason popular during his life. Like Hyppolite, he emphasized the variety of systems of thought and the importance of historical context. The argument about power that Foucault presents in *Discipline and Punish* is key to the book's philosophical claims that reason is historically contingent (that is, based on the ideas of a particular period). According to this view, what may be understood as reasonable, rational, or logical in one age may be considered unreasonable, irrational, or illogical in another. Foucault especially critiques understandings of rationality as something toward which humanity has steadily progressed. He demonstrates the way in which punishment has evolved—from the horrendous spectacle of the gallows to a system that controls and corrects behavior through a variety of forceful methods. In this way,

Foucault questions the idea that there has been a steady march of progress toward greater human reason.

Foucault's ideas on the ways in which power is exercised (through the creation of "knowledge" about a person) differs from the materialist interpretation of power in leftist Marxist thought that was so widespread in France at the time. His interpretation of power as "capillary,"[2] meaning that it is always present, even in everyday practices, was opposed to the Marxist econometric* analyses (interpretations of statistical economic data) that saw power as something rooted in material exploitation and the top-down authority of powerful elites.

NOTES

1   Didier Eribon, *Michel Foucault et ses contemporains* (Paris: Fayard, 1994), 155–86.

2   Michel Foucault, *Discipline and Punish: The Birth of the Prison* (Sheridan, NY: Vintage Books, 1979): 198.

THE AUTHOR'S CONTRIBUTION

KEY POINTS

- Michel Foucault's *Discipline and Punish* sought to trace the history of modern power relations by looking at eighteenth-century prisons and their development into the modern penal system.

- For Foucault, power operates through "power-knowledge,"* which classifies individuals and regulates the movements of their body in time and space through discipline.*

- Unlike the Marxist* thinkers of his time, who focused on how power was based on economic and class position, Foucault looked at the language and mechanisms of power.

Author's Aims

In a series of interviews conducted shortly before his death, Michel Foucault explained that the underlying aim of *Discipline and Punish: The Birth of the Prison* was not to develop a theory of power so much as to understand the history of modern power relations.[1] In the work of the economist and political theorist Karl Marx,* power is exercised by those with economic power; economics* determines who has power. For Foucault, however, power is primary and is not determined by economic position. While in a Marxist political–economic analysis, power is used to repress opposition or to forbid actions, in Foucault's work, power creates: it creates individuals, and social understandings of what those individuals are.

The goal of *Discipline and Punish* is, then, to trace a pattern of power relations as they existed in the eighteenth-century prison. By doing so, Foucault aimed to study the ideas of reason, the body, and the

> ❝ I am not developing a theory of power. I am working on the history, at a given moment, of the way reflexivity of self upon self is established, and the discourse of truth that is linked to it. When I speak about institutions of confinement in the eighteenth century, I am speaking about power relations as they existed at the time. ❞
>
> Michel Foucault, in *Critique and Power: Recasting the Foucault/Habermas Debate*

discussions of what was rational and right that developed during that time, and to trace how these ideas have developed up to today. The power relations within the prison help us to understand the makeup of the individual, which in turn helps us to understand how power operates and why it is effective.

In discussing these ideas, Foucault overturned social scientists' ideas of power and rationality* through a critique of Enlightenment* ideas regarding reason and an account of the ways in which knowledge is historically constructed.

Approach

Foucault's study of punishment turns on three main, interlinked ideas, which, he argues, form the basis of any regime: power, knowledge, and the body.

Although Foucault has a reputation for continually saying what power is *not* rather than defining what power *is*, it is worth noting that, for Foucault, power is not understood as something that can be possessed; it is something that creates and operates within social relationships. It is not something that one owns or holds, but rather something one exercises. Power is something that occurs in the tiniest interactions. Power is not the same as conflict or open domination. Power is, rather, productive; it acts through and forms individuals, instead of operating in opposition to their natural or preexisting will.

It is important to remember that *Discipline and Punish* is not concerned with how power operates in relation to specific politics or people. It is concerned with understanding how power operates in modern society and how this type of power came to be.

Foucault describes how the techniques of power depend on an "understanding" of their target. To control something, or someone, one must have "knowledge" of it. "Understanding" and "knowledge" here mean classifying the individual into one of several possible slots. For example, schools and universities keep transcripts of students' grades. In the act of doing so, they are classifying young people as "A," "B," or "C" students and thus creating "knowledge" about the kind of individual each student is. Instead of contesting a "B" grade, and thus the university's classification of them, a student may work harder in order to earn an "A" grade. In this way, the school or university is exercising power over the student. Power and knowledge, then, are deeply interrelated and depend on each other. Foucault's term "power-knowledge"[2] is intended to stress this interconnection.

Finally, Foucault understands the human body as a key target for applying power-knowledge. Institutions create "docile bodies"[3] that self-regulate in order to line up with the norms that are transmitted to them. For example, the soldier walks, talks, and stands in a certain way and through these bodily actions, signals he is lining up with the norms that the army gives him.

For Foucault, power operates through discipline. "Discipline" differs here from its common, everyday use. It refers to a mechanism of power that regulates individuals by acting upon the body in different ways. Discipline may place individuals in different spaces, by assigning them a particular room or cell in a building. It may control them in time, by providing them with a timetable that directs their movements throughout their day. Foucault is careful to make a distinction between discipline on the one hand, and power or punishment on the other.

Discipline is not power or punishment as we may understand it. It is, rather, a means by which power operates.

Using these ideas together, Foucault sees the history of punishment as a web of social relations that developed among "power-knowledge"[4] regimes and the human body.

Contribution in Context

In *Discipline and Punish*, Foucault distances himself from structuralism,* phenomenology,* and Marxism—the three schools with which his work was most often associated. His output differed from that of the Marxist scholars of his time in that it did not examine power from an economic point of view, or investigate relations among social classes. The concern, throughout *Discipline and Punish*, is with disciplinary structures, as opposed to economic ones. Similarly, Foucault's genealogy* represented an important break from the fields of phenomenology and structuralism.

Phenomenology and structuralism focus on the structures that allow certain knowledge or beliefs to exist. Foucault's genealogical approach did not concern itself with describing the content of a "knowledge" or belief system. Instead, he was concerned with the mechanisms by which a particular "knowledge" or system of beliefs comes into being. In other words, he is concerned with how a given "truth" is created. Foucault terms this process, and its inner workings, the "politics of the discursive regime"[5]—by which he means that the language we use to represent things is a product and source of power.

NOTES

1 Michael Kelly et al., *Critique and Power: Recasting the Foucault/Habermas Debate* (Cambridge, Mass.; London: MIT Press, 1994), 129.

2 Michel Foucault, *Discipline and Punish: The Birth of the Prison* (Sheridan, NY: Vintage Books, 1979), 27.

3 Foucault, *Discipline and Punish*, 135.

4   Foucault, *Discipline and Punish*, 27.

5   Michel Foucault, *Power/Knowledge: Selected Interviews and Other Writings, 1972–1977* (New York: Random House Digital, 1980), 118.

SECTION 2
IDEAS

MAIN IDEAS

KEY POINTS

- Foucault's *Discipline and Punish* examines how the rise of the modern prison reflects changes in the exercise of state power over society in general.

- For Foucault, starting in the eighteenth century, states moved from relying on punishment meant to torture and humiliate the body to a more elaborate system of constant control and correction of behavior.

- Foucault refused to follow any particular philosophical category. His writing is considered difficult to read, but he has had a big impact on the social sciences, which have adopted terms he invented, such as "power-knowledge,"* as part of their scholarly vocabulary.

Key Themes

Michel Foucault's *Discipline and Punish: The Birth of the Prison* is concerned with how the evolution of the modern penal system relates to the organization of society at large. Foucault argues that changes in the way states exercised power in the eighteenth century reflect alterations in the structure of society itself, with a shift from a setup of physical and often public punishment to a system of control and correction. We see, he writes, the emergence of prisons tasked with reshaping their subjects; in short, there was a shift from punishment to correction.

This shift had a deep effect on society. Foucault shows this by examining how the correctional methods of the prison bled into society at large, and were used in schools, hospitals, and, eventually, the

> ❝ Basically, I have only one object of historical study, that is the threshold of modernity. ❞
>
> Michel Foucault, *Michel Foucault, entretiens*

social sciences themselves. He argues that sociology* and philosophy* as we know them today are rooted in the practices of the first prisons. In the broadest sense, then, *Discipline and Punish*'s main themes are the institutional transformation of power, the rise of a disciplinary regime over society, and the relationship this new form of power has to academic fields including Foucault's own specialty.

This is also a work concerned with the dehumanizing* effects of modern power regimes (that is, the way that modern power regimes strip the individual of their human status, particularly in the light of the assumption that it is less complicated to exercise power on an individual who is not "really human"). Foucault is looking to expose the ways in which we discipline* ourselves, on a daily basis, into being certain kinds of individuals.

Foucault argues that the birth of the modern prison served to create the criminal. With the emergence of the prison, criminals now existed in society in ways that they never had before. First, because criminal offenders were so stigmatized (branded as criminals) and typically released without skills, they often reoffended, and fell into a pattern of career criminality. Second, and more importantly, he argues that the prison produces the criminal by creating a specific social category of the "individual criminal."

This can be called the epistemological production of the criminal.

Epistemology* is the study of the origins of knowledge and its limits, and the expression here refers to the systems of knowledge by which the criminal is known—all the ways in which inmates' behavior is tracked, measured, and judged in relation to their original crime and as part of the efforts to reform them. In other words, the penal institution gives rise to the criminal as an identifiable social category—a category of persons known only for the things they have done that society labels as wrong, and the measures being taken to ensure they do not do them again. Foucault argues that putting people in such a category is dehumanizing as it reduces the individual to a list of vital statistics.

In summary, there is a shift from understanding a crime-committing individual as an "individual-who-has-committed-a-crime" to understanding such an individual as a "criminal."

Exploring the Ideas

Discipline and Punish opens with the description of two contrasting types of punishment, each of which, Foucault says, represents the penal style of their period. Early forms of punishment sought to shame the body of offenders, he writes; modern forms seek to produce "normality" and conformism.

His first example is a graphic tale of a case of capital punishment—the execution of a man who had attempted to kill the French king in 1757. He was torn limb from limb before a large crowd in a display of ceremonial violence supervised by the state. Foucault sees this instance as typical of a now-outdated style of punishment, which relied on avenging the crime by humiliating the offender's body.

The second story is of a timetable in a Paris reformatory school eight years later. The reformatory operates on a strict and structured schedule that regulates the lives of its inmates: this regime decides all of the inmates' movements, including when and how much they can eat, sleep, exercise, or wash. In this second scenario, punishment occurs silently, without spectacle or ceremony. The goal is not vengeance, but reform: to reclaim the offenders' souls. Controlling their actions and where they can be ultimately leads to changing their behavior.

For Foucault, this shift toward systems of control that rely on knowledge rather than physical force has deep and wide-reaching implications. The methods and aims of these are symbolic of modern power relations: open violence and coercion* have been replaced by an exercise of power that relies on detailed knowledge of citizens, and long-term intervention intended to correct behavior. As Foucault puts it: "The idea is now to regulate thoroughly and at all times rather than to repress in fits and starts and, by this means, to improve troublesome individuals."[1] For Foucault, this shift from physical punishment to monitoring, measuring, and behavior-correcting marks the beginning of modernity*—the historical period in which we find ourselves today.

Language and Expression

Foucault's arguments are long and complicated and dependent on a very careful examination of aspects that society takes for granted. He is known among scholars for the intricacy and difficulty of his writing style, and his ideas can be hard to follow, even in English translation.

This difficulty may be due, in part, to his obvious efforts to evade being classified. While philosophers generally write in a specific tradition, or anchor their ideas in a specific framework, Foucault sets out, from the beginning of his work, to sketch out a new methodology, refusing to be identified with any one school of thought. Scholars such as the sociologist David Garland have noted that "the literary and rhetorical style in which he formulates his arguments, and the unfamiliarity of the new terms and concepts which litter the text" have earned *Discipline and Punish* a "certain notoriety" among scholars as being both slippery and impenetrable.[2]

This same notoriety, however, has certainly fueled the academic debate around his work. Much of the vocabulary he introduces in the text has since been adopted by philosophers, historians, sociologists, and cultural theorists, and terms such as power-knowledge, "governmentality,"* and "*le regard*"* ("the gaze")[3] have become quite common in discussions about power relations.

NOTES

1   David Garland, "Foucault's *Discipline and Punish*—An Exposition and Critique," *Law & Social Inquiry* 11, no. 4 (1986): 851.

2   Garland, "Foucault's *Discipline and Punish*": 847.

3   Michel Foucault, *Discipline and Punish*: *The Birth of the Prison* (Sheridan, NY: Vintage Books, 1979), 96.

MODULE 6
SECONDARY IDEAS

KEY POINTS

- Foucault believes modern social structures, including the family, schools, and workplaces, rely on the disciplinary methods of the modern prison. Self-governance by prisoners or citizens who have internalized the rules is crucial.

- Modern society exists, for Foucault, in a "carceral continuum"* in which government pressures people to regulate themselves. This idea influences discussions on education and prison reform.

- An underdeveloped and overlooked aspect of *Discipline and Punish* is Foucault's understanding of "the soul."

Other Ideas

Michel Foucault's *Discipline and Punish: The Birth of the Prison* can also be read as a commentary on the social organization of the family, on the workings of modern educational institutions, and, more generally, on the project of self-governance. He shows the ways in which institutions of social organization such as schools, universities, families, and workplaces have become increasingly subject to the disciplinary techniques of the prison.

Self-governance is crucial to his later works on what he calls "governmentality"*—the methods of regulation that work to get individuals to follow certain behaviors (the "conduct of conduct").[1] In other words, it refers to the ways in which governments seek to produce "ideal" citizens who will follow their rules. "Governmentality" is an important concept, and Foucault develops it in his subsequent texts, including the lectures to the College de France collected in

> **❝** One must remember that power is not an ensemble of mechanisms of negation, refusal, exclusion. But it produces effectively. It is likely that it produces right down to individuals themselves. **❞**
>
> Michel Foucault, *Michel Foucault, entretiens*

Security, Territory, Population [2] and the essay "Governmentality" published in *The Foucault Effect: Studies in Governmentality*.[3]

While less extensively studied than his analysis of panopticism* (the idea that prisoners, or ordinary citizens, can be brought to regulate their own behavior if they know they are being observed), Foucault's understanding of the overlap between modern methods of imprisonment and other social institutions and his concept of "governmentality" are important contributions to the study of power relations (the way in which power is distributed and enforced between different sections of a society).

Exploring the Ideas

Foucault, we remember, is concerned with understanding the relationship between carceral* institutions (prisons) and self-governance: "He who is subjected to a field of visibility [being observed], and who knows it," argues Foucault, "assumes responsibility for the constraints of power; he makes them play spontaneously upon himself; he inscribed in himself the power relation in which he simultaneously plays both roles, he becomes the principle of his own subjection."[4]

Studying the history of the modern prison and analyzing the effects of surveillance* on inmates' behavior led Foucault to think about how much other modern institutions depend on self-governance. Modern society relies heavily on getting its citizens used to behaving as if someone might be watching. In this sense, government includes not only formal state structures, but also "problems of self-control, guidance for the family and for children, management of the household, directing the soul, etc."[5]

"Government" operates through decentralized power, and is based on training or pressuring citizens to govern themselves. Placing warning labels on the negative health effects of smoking on cigarette packets is an example of "governmentality." Cigarettes are not banned, and the government does not punish individuals who smoke. And through regulatory measures such as warning labels, norms for behavior are subtly communicated to individuals and they are invited to behave in a certain way. Such a system relies on "instructing" individuals to self-govern. Foucault used this concept to describe advanced liberal democracies (the model on which the majority of Western democracies are based), and argues that in these systems, institutions such as schools and hospitals play a powerful normalizing role.[6] This idea has an influence on contemporary debates around education, prison reform, and public policy.

The other important subtheme in Foucault's work is his understanding of how bodies and people are governed through a process he terms "control of activity."[7] For example, the timetable in a prison or a reform school divides time in a disciplinary fashion, enabling time to penetrate the body completely, and controlling it totally by regimenting all the hours of the day. The timetable is accompanied by a technology of physical efficiency. Mechanisms of surveillance and discipline define each of the relationships between the body and the objects that it encounters. One sees this not just in prisons or reform schools but also in, say, the modern workplace, where one may fear receiving a disapproving glance from a manager or coworker for taking a long lunch, for leaving early, or for doing non-work activities while in the office. The office worker, upon being confronted with the possibility that the manager will see him or her leaving early, may self-regulate such behavior.

Foucault uses these examples to illustrate that a "carceral continuum"*[8] covers the entire pattern of social organization. This continuum is identifiable by a pressing concern with the identification of the anomalous—that which is out of place or not following the rules—and with abnormalities. This framework identifies the most minor infraction with the most major crime, and applies the same disciplinary mechanisms to all.

Overlooked

One aspect of the work has remained largely under-studied: Foucault's understanding of the "soul." Although Foucault himself claims that one of his projects in *Discipline and Punish* is to present a "genealogy*" of the modern soul,"[9] the text focuses on the networks of power that shape the soul, not the soul itself.

Foucault's idea of "soul," which refers to the term as it is used in the Judeo-Christian traditions, is linked to his other arguments on knowledge and power because it pushes aside and replaces the body as the focus of penal reform and surveillance. But critically, Foucault's emphasis on the soul is due to the modern processes of discipline that have structured and created that soul. Without discipline, surveillance, and the human sciences (including the mechanisms of observation and examination central to criminology*—the study of matters related to crime and criminal behavior—and the sciences of psychology* and psychiatry*), the normal soul as such would not exist.

"This real, non-corporal soul is not a substance; it is the element in which are articulated the effects of a certain type of power and the reference of a certain type of knowledge,"[10] Foucault writes. In contrast to the traditional Judeo-Christian conception of the body as the prison of the soul, he takes the soul to be the "prison of the body."[11]

This concept has been used to anchor others' investigations of modern identity. For example, the influential social theorist Nikolas

Rose* uses it as a starting point in his book *Governing the Soul*. The book first traces the development of some of the more important ideas in psychological practice in the twentieth century, and then attempts analytically to stretch psychology into economic life in much the way that Foucault does: by examining the way that social experts shape our lives and self-understandings. Such forces are an attempt to line up political and social goals of governance with individual-level desires, pleasures, and feelings; it is a meeting of institutional goals through self-fulfillment.[12]

NOTES

1   Graham Burchell et al., eds., *The Foucault Effect: Studies in Governmentality* (Chicago, IL: University of Chicago Press, 1991), 2.

2   Michel Foucault, *Security, Territory, Population, Lectures to the Collège de France, 1977–78* (London and New York: Palgrave MacMillan, 2007).

3   Burchell et al., T*he Foucault Effect*.

4   Michel Foucault, *Discipline and Punish: The Birth of the Prison* (Sheridan, NY: Vintage Books, 1979), 202–3

5   Thomas Lemke, "'The Birth of Bio-politics': Michel Foucault's Lecture at the Collège De France on Neo-liberal Governmentality," *Economy and Society* 30, no. 2 (2001): 2.

6   Michel Foucault, "Governmentality," in *The Essential Foucault*, ed. Paul Rabinow and Nikolas Rose (New York and London: The New Press, 2003), 102–3.

7   Foucault, *Discipline and Punish*, 149.

8   Foucault, *Discipline and Punish*, 293.

9   Foucault, *Discipline and Punish*, 23.

10 Foucault, *Discipline and Punish*, 29.

11 Foucault, *Discipline and Punish*, 29.

12 Nikolas Rose, *Governing the Soul: The Shaping of the Private Self* (Florence, KY: Taylor & Francis/Routledge, 1990), 258.

ACHIEVEMENT

KEY POINTS

- Michel Foucault's *Discipline and Punish* radically redefined the way sociologists and philosophers thought about modern power relations and their role in shaping society, culture, and identity.

- Its reception was influenced by its sociopolitical context: the radical French politics of the 1960s and 1970s, which his work reflected.

- Despite its positive reception, *Discipline and Punish* has not been without its critics. The sociologist Zygmunt Bauman,* for example, says today that most people are seduced, and not coerced, into following society's norms.

Assessing the Argument

Michel Foucault's *Discipline and Punish* attempted to illustrate the evolution of the power of modern institutions through the history of the modern penal system. By tracing the story of the modern prison, and showing the shift from public displays of punishment to systems of correction through means of observation and control, Foucault demonstrated the relationship between power, knowledge, the individual, and conformity. The key difference between ancient or feudal and modern styles of punishment is that modern institutions seek to reform the offender. Through monitoring and control, the system is able to mold a person to its liking, ensuring he or she conforms to a particular set of criteria. A system that gathers knowledge about its subjects can gain insight into their behavior and the reasons behind it, and make regulations to encourage individuals to self-regulate.

> 66 This book is intended as a correlative history of the modern soul and of a new power to judge. 99
>
> Michel Foucault, *Discipline and Punish: The Birth of the Prison*

Foucault demonstrates the wide-reaching implications of this new form of power. The workings of our schools, hospitals, factories, and offices all rely on the same principles of surveillance* and knowledge-gathering that constitute the modern prison. Moreover, the social sciences and their practices of data-gathering, subject-monitoring, and condition-diagnosing are rooted in these same ideas: academic thought in the sciences and humanities owes its existence to the principles of modern disciplinary regimes.

Achievement in Context

Foucault's work radically redefined the fields of philosophy* and sociology,* and particularly influenced the sociology of punishment,* a subdiscipline of sociology that explores the relationship between punishment and society. Until the publication of *Discipline and Punish*, this subdiscipline had relied heavily on the ideas of Emile Durkheim,*[1] the late nineteenth- and early twentieth-century founder of sociology, who emphasized the role of social institutions and social structure in organizing social life. Until the 1970s, the study of punishment remained largely the remit of criminologists* (scholars of crime and criminals) and penologists* (scholars of punishment and prisons), who approached it as a technical issue rather than a sociological one. In other words, they focused on how to punish more effectively, instead of focusing on the history and implications of the forms of punishment imposed by institutions.

In this sense, Foucault's work both helped to redefine the scope of intellectual thought in his field and developed a new approach for understanding power relations across multiple disciplines.

Beyond its specific contributions, the book's critical reception was also clearly helped by the sociopolitical climate of the time. The radical politics of the late 1960s and early 1970s, which included the student protests in Paris in May 1968,* opposition to the Vietnam War,* and anti-colonialist sentiment among French intellectuals, made Foucault's ideas intensely relevant for his readers at the time. His understanding of the way power and knowledge work together to create conformity found a ready audience in intellectuals unhappy with the state of the French education system, the seeming elitism of academia, and the country's role in oppressing its colonies.*

Limitations

First published in 1975, *Discipline and Punish* spoke to many of the sociopolitical concerns of its time, and it is often regarded as reflecting French leftist sentiment of the 1960s and 1970s. What makes it a key work across the humanities and social sciences, however, is that it can be applied beyond that period, and beyond the disciplines of sociology, philosophy, and history from which it emerged. Foucault's historical approach, which traces the story of punishment from the Middle Ages to modernity* (the modern period), and which identifies the first instances of modern discipline,* is specifically designed to provide a way of understanding power in various contexts, and across various historical periods.

In the text, Foucault's concern is not with the mechanisms of power in France in the 1960s and 1970s, but rather with the workings of modern power in the abstract: how power works in any modern context. His central ideas—the role of surveillance, control, and knowledge-gathering—can be applied to a variety of different settings, and are not limited to specific forms of governance. So, for example, his ideas remain acutely relevant to the concerns of twenty-first-century readers living in a neoliberal* globalized* economy, since this system, too, relies on surveillance mechanisms, data-gathering, and monitoring of its citizens. ("Neoliberal" here refers to the current economic orthodoxy that the route to economic growth lies through unregulated free trade, privatization, and the smallest amount of governmental intervention possible, and so on; "globalization" refers to the increasing convergence of the world's economies and cultures.) In fact, in light of technological developments such as the Internet and closed-circuit television (CCTV)*—which did not exist in Foucault's time—one might even argue that the ideas expressed in *Discipline and Punish* are more relevant now than when the book was first published. This is one reason why it is regularly used today in scholarship on digital culture.*

Despite *Discipline and Punish's* positive reception, it has not been immune to criticism. The leading sociologist Zygmunt Bauman, for example, argues that disciplinary society marked a certain moment in modernity in which large layers of the population needed to be regulated efficiently. This was the age of the army and the factory. Disciplinary society, however, as Foucault formulated it, is less relevant in post-modern society. For Bauman, "The great majority of people … are today integrated through seduction rather than policing, advertising rather than indoctrinating, need-creation rather than normative regulation."[2] In other words, we are seduced, rather than monitored into being certain kinds of subjects. We desire to, for example, be fit and healthy individuals not because we are being watched by the authorities, but because advertising seduces us into wanting to be fit and healthy.

NOTES

1   See: Emile Durkheim and Lewis A. Coser, *The Division of Labor in Society* (New York, NY: Free Press, 1997).

2   Zygmunt Bauman, "On Postmodern Uses of Sex," *Theory, Culture & Society* 15, no. 3 (1998): 23.

PLACE IN THE AUTHOR'S WORK

KEY POINTS

- Michel Foucault explored the relationship between history, normality, and abnormality throughout his career. He was particularly concerned with how institutions impose certain norms of behavior by branding people who step out of line.

- *Discipline and Punish* was among Foucault's last published works, and is viewed by scholars as marking the beginning of his "genealogical"* phase, which they distinguish from his earlier "archaeological"* phase.

- The text has remained relevant through the changing relationships between the state and its citizens, first under the welfare state* (in which the government ensures a degree of security for its citizens) and then neoliberalism* (in which the government intervenes as little as possible in the economic lives of its citizens).

Positioning

Discipline and Punish: The Birth of the Prison is a product of Michel Foucault's long concern with the role played by labels such as "madness" or "criminality" in creating and maintaining structures of power, and in the ways norms for behavior are communicated to citizens. In *Madness and Civilization* (1961), for example, Foucault distinguishes mental illness from "madness." He argues that the latter is a social construct used by institutions to brand people who deviate from the norm. As with his later publications, his 1961 book takes a historical approach, using the history of medicine to critique modern assumptions about mental health and so-called "normality."

> ❝ If you are not like everybody else, then you are abnormal; if you are abnormal, then you are sick. These three categories, not being like everybody else, not being normal and being sick are in fact very different but they have been reduced to the same thing. ❞
>
> Michel Foucault, *Michel Foucault, entretiens*

Foucault's later works, *The Birth of the Clinic* (1963) and *The Order of Things* (1966), extended some of these ideas. *The Birth of the Clinic* traced the history of medicine from the late eighteenth and early nineteenth centuries, a period of huge transformation and radical development of new technologies. *The Order of Things* examined science as a whole, arguing that throughout history, scientific discourse has had to accept certain assumptions as the "truth"—but that these so-called facts have differed from era to era.

Foucault began writing *Discipline and Punish* in the late 1960s, and the work represents a later stage in his intellectual life. Foucault himself often referred to the text as his "first book"[1] because he thought it the one that most fully and faithfully developed his thought. It also served as a bridge to his later ideas; for example, while Foucault first mentioned "governmentality"* in *Discipline and Punish*, he developed it more fully in later works.

Integration

Although *Discipline and Punish* brings together concepts that concerned Foucault throughout his life—such as history,* power-knowledge,* normalization,* and self-governance*—it also marks a departure from his previous work. The study is his first effort to apply a "genealogical" approach to history, as opposed to the "archaeological" approach of his previous historical projects. These methods differ in several important ways.

An archaeological approach is based on the idea that systems of thought are regulated by subconscious mechanisms within individuals. It seeks to place and explore systems of knowledge in relation to the conditions from which they emerged. As such, it can be thought of as an exploration of possibilities: of the creation of the potentials that shape thought. Unlike both the philosophical approach of phenomenology* and traditional history, an archaeological method does not draw on expressions of individual psychology*; rather, it looks at how thoughts, ideas, and discursive* practices—culturally and historically specific rules for producing knowledge—are formed. That said, archaeology can compare only different discursive practices and ways of knowing that operate at different times or in different contexts. It is not equipped to articulate the *causes* of changes in thinking or the variations in discursive practice.

Foucault's concept of genealogy was intended to remedy this theoretical and methodological shortcoming. The term itself was a reference to Friedrich Nietzsche's* "genealogy of morals." By using a genealogical approach, *Discipline and Punish* aimed to demonstrate that any given system of knowledge or thinking was the result of historically contingent* events—the result of the history that came before it. In other words, genealogy is a way of explaining the present by placing it in relation to the past. Foucault's genealogical approach is concerned with the mechanisms by which a particular science or system of beliefs comes into being—which is also to say, how a given "truth" is created. Foucault terms this process, and its inner workings, the "politics of the discursive regime."[2] In broader terms, then, the text extends Foucault's life-long concern with questioning the very discourse of philosophy* itself, and challenging what he saw as its uncritical tendencies.

Significance

Foucault's *Discipline and Punish* turned out to be more useful than perhaps even he had expected, as its ideas have remained valid even as the socioeconomic landscape of the West has changed. Foucault worked on the text in the 1960s and through the 1970s, just as the Bretton Woods* international monetary system was abandoned and, along with it, the financial philosophies that provided the theoretical foundation for the welfare state.

Bretton Woods was a system of monetary management that regulated commercial and financial relationships among the major industrial economies from just after World War II until the early 1970s. The system allowed governments to play a greater role in international and national power relations than that which we experience today. The "welfare state" refers to the many government-funded institutions and programs that provide care to a state's citizens—including health care, social security, and other social benefits.

Under these two regimes, the dynamics described by Foucault would occur between government officials and citizens: between a social worker and a youth offender, for example, or between a psychologist and a patient, or a parole officer and his or her charge. Foucault's primary concern was with the disciplinary mechanisms used by these state initiatives. The point underlying his critique was that specialties such as social work and health care, which we assume to be progressive, apolitical, and benevolent, are, in fact, involved with the subjugation,* surveillance,* and control of citizens.

These same ideas, however, turned out also to be widely valid under neoliberalism, the economic regime that took the place of Bretton Woods, and which exists to this day. Neoliberalism is a set of economic policies that promotes economic liberalization, free trade, open markets, privatization, deregulation, and strengthening of the role of the private sector, and it has proven to raise similar concerns about surveillance, individual privacy, and choice as the system it replaced.[3] In this sense, then, *Discipline and Punish* has been effective, remaining relevant to the concerns of scholars and critics in the globalized* world today.

It is also thanks to this timelessness and universality that the text has had such a far-reaching influence. Its examination of the relationship between power, knowledge, surveillance, and the individual are relevant to contemporary discussions about privacy, data-collection, and the spread and use of information in the digital age. As well as radically redefining the fields of sociology and philosophy, *Discipline and Punish* has since proven a useful document for understanding power relations today.

NOTES

1   James Miller, *The Passion of Michel Foucault* (Cambridge, MA: Harvard University Press, 1993).

2   Michel Foucault, *Power/Knowledge: Selected Interviews and Other Writings*, 1972–1977 (New York: Random House Digital, 1980), 118.

3   Nancy Fraser, "From Discipline to Flexibilization? Rereading Foucault in the Shadow of Globalization," *Constellations* 10, no. 2 (2003): 160–71.

SECTION 3
IMPACT

MODULE 9
THE FIRST RESPONSES

KEY POINTS

- Michel Foucault's *Discipline and Punish* was met with criticism after its publication, most famously from the social scientist and philosopher Jürgen Habermas,* who took issue with Foucault's critique of the thinking of the period of European intellectual history known as the Enlightenment* and his claim that reason itself is socially constructed.

- Foucault and Habermas engaged in a debate over these issues throughout the last years of Foucault's life.

- *Discipline and Punish* has also been criticized for being an inaccurate representation of how power works in prisons.

Criticism

Michel Foucault's *Discipline and Punish* inspired intense criticism when it was first published. The most famous came from Jürgen Habermas, a highly regarded social scientist and philosopher. Habermas's critique and the debate that followed, which is known among scholars as the "Foucault–Habermas debate," engaged both thinkers for a number of years, and spanned a number of their works.

Habermas has been the strongest contemporary defender of the Enlightenment's faith in reason, approaching power from a radically different point of view: from what he terms "communicative rationality"* and "discourse* ethics."[1] By this he means, roughly, that reason is possible and is the outcome of successful communication. While Foucault argues that there is no fixed human character, and that reason is historically produced and contingent*

> ❝ The constant division between the normal and the abnormal, to which every individual is subjected, brings us back to our own time, by applying the binary branding and exile of the leper to quite different objects; the existence of the whole set of techniques and institutions for measuring, supervising and correcting the abnormal brings into play the disciplinary mechanisms to which the fear of the plague gave rise. ❞
>
> Michel Foucault, *Discipline and Punish: The Birth of the Prison*

(that is, its historical context is crucial), Habermas contends that there is a fixed human character, and that reason can solve human dilemmas.

Second, Habermas argues that only practices which produce free communication can generate legitimate social organization. The whole idea of this theory is deeply at odds with Foucault, as it differs from Foucault's claim that social interaction itself is always structured and constrained by power. Further, he argues that Foucault wrongly reduces all culture and politics to violence, and social life to a series of power interactions.

Habermas and Foucault were also in conflict in their methodological approach. Habermas accuses Foucault of being "utterly unsociological," which is to say that Foucault did not follow the scientific method.[2] Other critics, such as the political philosopher Nancy Fraser,* have criticized Foucault's work on similar lines; Foucault, Fraser argues, encourages us to criticize modern society while telling us that criticism is pointless as we cannot escape from power.

Responses

One of Foucault's most famous responses to Habermas appears in the essay "What is Enlightenment?" written toward the end of his life. In this essay, Foucault argues that modernity* and the Enlightenment are attitudes, rather than periods in history. The goal is not to find universal human values or characteristics but, rather, to understand how it is we came to be. Further, instead of searching for a basic humanity, we should instead consider the kind of selves we want to be.

Foucault insists that his perspective on truth and power contains more nuances than Habermas supposes. Instead of being a critique of the possibility of reason or rationality,* Foucault saw his work as a study of the practice of contrasting rationality with irrationality. For Foucault, his whole project seeks to demonstrate that the use of those two categories themselves—and their placement in a hierarchy—is too simplistic.

Foucault also argues against Habermas's view that truth and reason are absolute—which is to say, that one is either in truth or in error. For Habermas, rationality is truth. There is only one truth, and there exists a precise distinction between truth and untruth. But Foucault considers this sort of dichotomy to be a form of "intellectual blackmail."[3] Reason, he argues, is deeply subjective: it is socially constructed (that is, a product of particular social circumstances), and dependent on historical and cultural contexts. For Foucault, "reason is self-created, which is why I have tried to analyze forms of rationality: different foundations, different creations, different modifications in which rationalities engender one another, oppose and pursue one another."[4] The process by which we come to assume certain things to be true, for him, is most worthy of our study: Foucault is interested in how particular systems of knowledge come about, and how those systems undermine or affirm existing power dynamics. The critique of knowledge itself—including our understanding of truth, and our processes of reflection—is a crucial part of his project.

Conflict and Consensus

In the four decades since its publication, aspects of *Discipline and Punish* have continued to attract controversy. For example, the political psychologist C. Fred Alford* has criticized what he sees as Foucault's methodological failings.[5] Drawing on his own ethnographic experience studying prisons in the United States, Alford argues that the disciplinary practices upon which Foucault develops his argument are, in fact, absent from modern prisons, and suggests that the opposite principle is visible. For Alford, discipline in prisons occurs through the control of entrances and exits rather than through the constant possibility of surveillance*—supervising entrances and exits renders surveillance irrelevant. Prison authorities don't watch prisoners, he argues, because their power is already shown in their ability to direct comings and goings. They have the power not to care enough to look. Alford claims that Foucault founds his arguments on theories and ideas about prisons that do not relate to the historical reality. For instance, the theoretical prison inside which inmates could never be certain they were unobserved, the Panopticon,* was never constructed—but writing as if these prison reforms took place, Foucault mistakes ideological claims for practice. This, further, confuses his understanding of power.

Voicing a relatively common critique of Foucault, Alford further criticizes him for writing as if the new disciplinary practices were completely different from older or more "traditional" modes of power. Alford argues, against Foucault, that disciplinary practices are indeed exercised by all rulers and authorities.

NOTES

1   Jürgen Habermas, *The Theory of Communicative Action, Vol. 1: Reason and the Rationalization of Society* (Boston, MA: Beacon Press, 1984).

2   Didier Eribon, *Michel Foucault et ses contemporains* (Paris: Fayard, 1994), 155–86.

3   Michel Foucault, "What Is Enlightenment?," in *The Foucault Effect: Studies in Governmentality*, ed. Graham Burchell et al. (Chicago, IL: University of Chicago Press, 1991), 42.

4   Quoted in Michael Kelly et al., *Critique and Power: Recasting the Foucault/ Habermas Debate* (Cambridge, Mass.; London: MIT Press, 1994), 119.

5   C. Fred Alford, "What Would It Matter if Everything Foucault Said About Prison Were Wrong? *Discipline and Punish* After Twenty Years," *Theory and Society* 29, no. 1 (2000): 125–46.

MODULE 10
THE EVOLVING DEBATE

KEY POINTS

- While scholars in a variety of disciplines have taken up the ideas in *Discipline and Punish*, even the book's basic assumptions have attracted sharp criticism.

- The text led to the development of the sociology of punishment* (the analysis of why and how we punish,) and has helped shape the vocabulary of numerous subfields of sociology, including organizational sociology* (a branch of sociology that looks at organizations) and sociology of law.*

- Scholars have found concepts of "power-knowledge"* and "discipline"* particularly useful.

Uses and Problems

Michel Foucault's *Discipline and Punish* remains a key text for sociologists and philosophers, theorists, social scientists, and scholars of the humanities. New writers following Foucault's lead have used the concepts found in *Discipline and Punish*, such as discipline and panopticism,* to chart the overlapping of power and the modern individual. Scholars have used Foucault's theoretical insights as a framework to examine a variety of issues that he could not have predicted, such as thinking about obesity[1] or human resource management.*[2]

That said, *Discipline and Punish* has not been free from criticism. In lectures he gave a few years after the publication of the text, collected in the book *Security, Territory, Population*, Foucault himself criticized the earlier work's overemphasis on discipline as a restriction on individual freedom. In a refinement of his earlier thought, Foucault argued that

> **❝** The human body was entering a machinery of power that explores it, breaks it down and rearranges it. A 'political anatomy', which was also a 'mechanics of power', was being born; it defined how one may have a hold over others' bodies, not only so that they may do what one wishes, but so that they may operate as one wishes, with the techniques, the speed and the efficiency that one determines. Thus discipline produces subjected and practiced bodies, 'docile' bodies. **❞**
>
> Michel Foucault, *Discipline and Punish: The Birth of the Prison*

we must conceive of power as something that thinks "of men's freedom, of what they want to do, of what they have an interest in doing, and of what they think about doing" and as "a regulation that can only be carried out through and by reliance on the freedom of each."[3] The social theorist Nikolas Rose* has developed these ideas further in *Powers of Freedom: Reframing Political Thought*,[4] which extends this argument in order to consider the ways in which individual freedom becomes a task of modern governance.

Other scholars have attempted to update his account of panopticism. The Norwegian sociologist Thomas Mathiesen, for instance, has argued that power lies not in the model of the Panopticon,* in which the few watch the many, but in what he calls the "Synopticon," in which the many watch the few. He argues that we live not in a disciplinary society but in a viewer society. He uses as evidence the rise of celebrity culture and the mass media, in which the general public—the "many"—model their behavior by watching the actions of "the few"—be they celebrities, politicians, or other public figures in current culture.[5]

Schools of Thought

From the late 1970s, a new variation of studies of carceral* institutions (places in which people are incarcerated) has begun to emerge, most of which now focus on the role of prisons in creating and maintaining a social order rather than on punishment itself. These new studies, broadly referred to as the sociology of punishment, rely on concepts found in Foucault's texts, including state control and the processes by which individuals are created as social subjects.

Foucault's work can be credited for this development in several ways. First, according to one scholar, Foucault "demonstrated to a wide audience of historians and social theorists the far-reaching sociological significance of punishment and the kinds of insights which might be gained from a close examination of its practices."[6] It also created an important set of tools for understanding state control. Foucault's ideas about penalty and criminal regulation have since been adopted and refined within the subdiscipline. These changes are important, and can be seen in the very language with which sociologists now discuss law, penalty, control, and state power: "Discipline," "surveillance,"* "power-knowledge," and "normalization"* are all routine parts of contemporary sociological vocabulary.

Sociologists of the law have followed suit,[7] attempting to create frameworks that understand law as governance and discipline; some scholars have even constructed what they term a "Foucauldian theory of the law," emphasizing the ways by which the law should be understood as a form of governance.

In Current Scholarship

The influence of *Discipline and Punish* has spread widely throughout the social sciences and humanities. Recently, the unlikely subfields of organizational sociology* and management have absorbed some of the key insights of the text—and the body of Foucault's work in general—with unusual applications to other areas of social science and social life. For example, the American social geographer and food scholar Julie Guthman uses the concept of "power-knowledge" to discuss how ideas of health interact with access to food to produce dramatically unequal societies.[8] The British management economist Barbara Townley,* meanwhile, argues that the practice of human resource management can be best understood as a discursive regime that renders employees governable through practices of subject-making similar to techniques deployed in the Panopticon.[9] Likewise, the organizational theorist Gibson Burrell's work looks at how organizations are mechanisms of surveillance and discipline.*[10]

With respect to organizational sociology and administrative science* in particular, *Discipline and Punish* remains a highly original contribution. Organizational sociology relies, in no small part, on concepts of rationality* and efficiency, and benefits dramatically (though often uncomfortably) from a Foucault-style analysis that questions the nature of power, governance, and the individuals involved.

NOTES

1 Julie Guthman and Melanie DuPuis, "Embodying Neoliberalism: Economy, Culture, and the Politics of Fat," *Environment and Planning D: Society and Space* 24, no. 3 (2006): 427–48.

2 Barbara Townley, "Foucault, Power/Knowledge, and Its Relevance for Human Resource Management," *The Academy of Management Review* 18, no. 3 (July 1993): 518–45.

3 Michel Foucault, Security, *Territory, Population, Lectures to the Collège de France 1977–1978* (London and New York: Palgrave Macmillan, 2007): 49.

4 Nikolas Rose, *Powers of Freedom: Reframing Political Thought* (Cambridge: Cambridge University Press, 1999).

5 Thomas Mathiesen, "The Viewer Society: Foucault's Panopticon Revisited," *Theoretical Criminology* 1, no. 2 (1997).

6 David Garland, "Frameworks of Inquiry in the Sociology of Punishment," *The British Journal of Sociology* 41, no. 1 (March 1990): 2.

7   See: Alan Hunt and Gary Wickham, *Foucault and Law: Towards a Sociology of Law as Governance* (Boulder, CO and London: Pluto Press, 1994).

8   Guthman and DuPuis, "Embodying Neoliberalism," 427–48.

9   Barbara Townley, "Foucault, Power/Knowledge, and Its Relevance for Human Resource Management," *The Academy of Management Review* 18, no. 3 (July 1993): 518–45.

10 Gibson Burrell, "Modernism, Post Modernism and Organizational Analysis 2: The Contribution of Michel Foucault," *Organization Studies* 9, no. 2 (April 1988): 221–35.

IMPACT AND INFLUENCE TODAY

KEY POINTS

- Michel Foucault's *Discipline and Punish* has become a core work both in its original fields of sociology* and history,* and in other humanities and social science disciplines.

- Foucault's ideas have been used to examine issues as varied as obesity, sexuality, ethics, and the epistemological* status of the state—that is, the place of the state according to theories of what can be known and how we come to know it.

- The Habermas–Foucault debates have continued, even after Foucault's death, as scholars continue to discuss the contrasting views of reason.

Position

Michel Foucault's *Discipline and Punish* remains a central text in diverse fields, especially in history, anthropology,* and sociology. Although there are variations, sociologists who follow Foucault focus largely on power, discourse* (for Foucault, a way of speaking that arises from the influence of history and power, but elsewhere a term signifying, roughly, the exchange of ideas that defines how something is understood), the body, and the creation of the individual. These are all themes that Foucault examined closely.

The organizational sociologist* Nancy Fraser,*[1] the political sociologist Barbara Townley,* and the development scholar James Ferguson[2] all use the concept of "discourse" in their work. Nancy Fraser in particular has written provocatively about how Foucault's thinking on discipline,* written in the 1950s and 1960s while governmental intervention in the economy and investment in the

> ❝ Is it surprising that prisons resemble factories, schools, barracks, and hospitals, which all resemble prisons? ❞
>
> Michel Foucault, *Discipline and Punish: The Birth of the Prison*

welfare state* formed economic orthodoxy, can be applied to the more globalized* neoliberal* state that exists today, where markets are left to their own devices and ensuring social justice and welfare is less of a priority. She explores his ideas of how the state and the market create discourses around self-governance. Similarly, sociologists of punishment and crime such as David Garland,[3] Joachim Savelsberg,[4] and John Braithwaite[5] have been influenced by Foucault's understanding of punishment as a form of social control.

A number of scholars have absorbed Foucault's work on the human body, adapting it for theoretical emphasis on matters as diverse as obesity,[6] feminist studies,*[7] queer theory*[8] (scholarly inquiry into gender and identity often conducted with a view to challenge traditional understandings of each), and the development of anatomical science.[9] These thinkers take their cue from Foucault's understanding of the body as the site of discipline and the target of disciplining technologies in order to think about how minority or marginalized groups are made to conform.

Meanwhile, theorists of the state such as Robert Jessop[10] and Thomas Lemke*[11] have applied Foucault's thinking to an analysis of government, including the centrality of "power-knowledge"*[12] and discursive practices (the production and organization of knowledge) within the state. For Jessop and Lemke, Foucault provides the basis for a theoretical understanding of technologies of governance. Foucault allows us, they say, to shift from seeing the state as a singular entity that governs from above, to seeing governance as being made up of the actions and practices of a varied set of actors. An example of the kind of shift of which they are talking could be government partnerships with non-profit organizations or charities that provide, for example, support for substance abusers or those who engage in other forms of deviant behavior. These practices often work on the basis of discipline—through individuals' self-regulation.

Interaction

Although *Discipline and Punish* studies history, sociology, criminology,* and cultural theory* it belongs to all and none of these genres, making it hard to place it in any one subdiscipline or tradition. For this reason, Foucault's theorizing has some of the broadest implications of any current thinker—which is why it has been interpreted across a number of different academic fields. For example, the anthropologist James Faubion has employed Foucault's thinking on social institutions in his study of ethics;[13] the classicist David Larmour has used his work in thinking on sexuality and antiquity;[14] and the historian Vazira Zamindar writes on boundaries and citizens using ideas of the creation of individual identities and discipline found in Foucault's work.[15]

What these very different Foucauldian scholars share is a tendency to seek out institutional histories, to identify social control, and to adopt methods that mimic Foucault's genealogy.* Foucault lends himself to such projects, since he provides a widely applicable method via which scholars can examine the flow of power and knowledge in any arena or historical context.

The Continuing Debate

Foucault and the sociologist Jürgen Habermas* had only just overcome the bitterness that had previously characterized their debate when Foucault died in 1984. So it fell to Foucault's followers to continue the discourse. The debate takes up the very nature of rationality* and, by extension, the possibility for human emancipation* (that is, liberation, as if from slavery). Scholars of reason and critical theory retain an active engagement in the Foucault–Habermas debate, as it speaks to a basic principle of social theory: whether or not human societies are by nature prone to conflict.

Scholars who follow Foucault have, by and large, dismissed Habermas's critique of Foucault's supposed relativism (that is, his supposed belief that there are no absolutes in certain matters) as invalid because it tends to "presuppose what it seeks to show."[16] Others have continued to argue that the Habermasian analysis is based on a misunderstanding of the substance of Foucault's work. These scholars include the likes of Michael Kelly, who defends Foucault, arguing that Habermas has misunderstood the ideas of both disciplinary power and local critique. Kelly says that although Foucault criticizes the dominant forms of rationality that have been present since the Enlightenment,* he at no time argues that reason itself is worthless.[17] And in their 1999 book, *Foucault contra Habermas: Recasting the Dialogue Between Genealogy and Critical Theory*, the sociologists Samantha Ashenden and David Owen attempt to breathe new life into the debate by providing a "Foucauldian rejoinder" to later Habermasian critiques.

NOTES

1   Nancy Fraser, "From Discipline to Flexibilization? Rereading Foucault in the Shadow of Globalization," *Constellations* 10, no. 2 (2003).

2   James Ferguson, *The Anti-politics Machine: Development, Depoliticization, and Bureaucratic Power in Lesotho* (Minneapolis: University of Minnesota Press, 1994).

3   See: David Garland, "Frameworks of Inquiry in the Sociology of Punishment," *The British Journal of Sociology* 41, no. 1 (March 1990).

4   Joachim J. Savelsberg, "Knowledge, Domination, and Criminal Punishment," *American Journal of Sociology* 99, no. 4 (January 1994): 911–43.

5   John Braithwaite, "What's Wrong with the Sociology of Punishment?" *Theoretical Criminology* 7, no. 1 (February 2003): 5–28.

6   Julie Guthman and Melanie DuPuis, "Embodying Neoliberalism: Economy, Culture, and the Politics of Fat," *Environment and Planning D: Society and Space* 24, no. 3 (2006): 427–48.

7   Jana Sawicki, *Disciplining Foucault: Feminism, Power, and the Body* (London: Routledge, 1991); Susan Hekman, ed., *Feminist Interpretations of Michel Foucault* (University Park, PA: Pennsylvania State University Press, 1996).

8   David Halperin, *Saint Foucault: Towards a Gay Hagiography* (Oxford and New York: Oxford University Press, 1997).

9   Jan C. Rupp, "Michel Foucault, Body Politics and the Rise and Expansion of Modern Anatomy," *Journal of Historical Sociology* 5, no. 1 (1992): 31–60.

10 Bob Jessop, "From Micro-powers to Governmentality: Foucault's Work on Statehood, State Formation, Statecraft and State Power," *Political Geography* 26, no. 1 (January 2007): 34–40.

11 Thomas Lemke, "An Indigestible Meal? Foucault, Governmentality and State Theory," *Distinktion, Scandinavian Journal of Social Theory* 8, no. 2 (2007): 43–64.

12 Michel Foucault. *Discipline and Punish: The Birth of the Prison* (Sheridan, NY: Vintage Books, 1979): 27.

13 James D. Faubion, "Toward an Anthropology of Ethics: Foucault and the Pedagogies of Autopoiesis," *Representations* 74, no. 1 (Spring 2001): 83–104.

14 David H. J. Larmour et al., *Rethinking Sexuality: Foucault and Classical Antiquity* (Princeton, NJ: Princeton University Press, 1997).

15 Vazira Fazila-Yacoobali Zamindar, *The Long Partition and the Making of Modern South Asia: Refugees, Boundaries, Histories* (New York, NY: Columbia University Press, 2007).

16 Samantha Ashenden and David Owen, *Foucault Contra Habermas: Recasting the Dialogue Between Genealogy and Critical Theory* (Thousand Oaks, CA; London: SAGE, 1999).

17 Michael Kelly et al., *Critique and Power: Recasting the Foucault/Habermas Debate* (Cambridge, MA; London: MIT Press, 1994), 372.

WHERE NEXT?

KEY POINTS

- Michel Foucault's *Discipline and Punish* remains an important text for humanities and social science scholars interested in modern power relations.

- The work has wide applications in contemporary discussions about digital surveillance* mechanisms and individual privacy. It has also had a marked influence in the sociology of health and illness.

- Foucault's study is timeless, as it examines the techniques and mechanisms used in power relations rather than explicitly attacking a specific group or institution's exercise of power.

Potential

Michel Foucault's *Discipline and Punish* remains a key text for scholars in the humanities and social sciences, and has wide applications beyond sociology,* in fields as diverse as international relations,* digital culture studies,* law, literary studies,* feminist* criticism, queer theory,* and cultural theory.* This in itself is something of a paradox, given that so much of Foucault's work was written as a critique of academic discourse, and was in opposition to the fields that have since absorbed him.

The way his work can be applied to the discussion of technologies that did not exist in his lifetime is a further tribute to its timelessness. It is remarkable to think that when Foucault wrote the words "visibility is a trap,"[1] CCTV* cameras and the Internet did not yet exist. In this sense, he anticipated with uncanny foresight some key aspects of the

> **❝ Visibility is a trap. ❞**
> Michel Foucault, *Discipline and Punish: The Birth of the Prison*

power relations of the world in which we live today. Indeed, Foucault's work has gained renewed attention in the past decade in scholarly and public debates about individual privacy in the digital age, and in discussions about power in neoliberal* globalized* economies. For example, the anti-capitalist scholars Michael Hardt* and Antonio Negri* argue that Foucault's work has "prepared the terrain for [...] an investigation of the material functioning of imperial rule."[2] Still, other parts of the leftist movement see Foucault's insistence that there is no absolute right and wrong as a curse, calling him a "crucial source of the malaise affecting the rest of the left—the gutless relativism which prevents [action]."[3]

His work is widely cited in discussions about digital surveillance, including, most recently, David M. Berry's *Critical Theory and the Digital* (2014),[4] and the fourth edition of Cynthia Weber's key guide to contemporary international relations* theory. Weber concisely explains the lasting relevance of Foucault's ideas in the digital age and shows the extent to which his ideas anticipated Edward Snowden's* disclosures of US government surveillance.[5] And in *Crime, Justice and the Media* (2009), Ian Marsh and Gaynor Melville examine the logical extension of these ideas, addressing the issue of how the circulation of certain types of information—including biased accounts of events—helps strengthen and maintain social control.[6] Finally, David Lyon's *Theorizing Surveillance* (2006) uses Foucault's ideas as a starting point for conceptualizing the role of surveillance in contemporary society. Each contributor in the collection examines surveillance from a Foucauldian, or anti-Foucauldian, point of view.[7]

Future Directions

Foucault's mark in the social sciences has been exceptionally powerful in the field of the sociology of health and illness. This is particularly noteworthy given that the sociology of health and illness has traditionally understood the body as a "natural" analytical starting point, whereas Foucault views the body and knowledge about it as "constructed." Foucault, in essence, sees medicine's understanding of the body as historically specific.[8] To apply his work here is thus to redefine the field's basic approach—a notable influence, to say the least. The leading sociologist of health, David Armstrong, has written provocatively about subjectivity within medicine,[9] identity within public health,[10] and the development of medical knowledge,[11] using Foucault's genealogical method.

The influential British sociologist Nikolas Rose* has stayed faithfully within the tradition of Foucault to write about the psychiatric sciences.[12] The sociologists William Ray Arney and Jane Neill have traced the transformation of the understanding of the pain of childbirth, claiming that obstetricians' comprehension of such pain altered alongside changes in the "power-knowledge"*[13] discourses of pain.[14] Deborah Lupton of the University of Canberra argues that public health practices, which are typically taken for granted as a neutral application of science, are in fact value-laden, socially subjective, and context-dependent.[15] Each of these analyses are openly Foucauldian, taking as a starting point both Foucault's methodological approach—genealogy*—and his political–economic treatment of power, surveillance, and subjectivity.

Outside of sociology, Foucault's ideas have shaped the work of urban theorists examining the ways in which citizens inhabit, and move through, the city and the role that surveillance plays in these activities. His beliefs have also influenced the work of queer theorists, who examine institutional efforts to enforce "traditional" values such as marriage to someone of the opposite sex. These studies start from

Foucault's premise that all government involves social engineering, and that the enforcement of heterosexuality is part of that project.

Summary
Foucault's enduring insights—that identities are not fixed and that power configurations are contextual—have proven useful tools to scholars across the disciplines. Foucauldian understandings of power, and Foucauldian concepts such as "discipline",* "power-knowledge,"[16] and "surveillance" have enriched the comprehension of power dynamics in various settings. His work provides a powerful bridge for understanding both the meaning of a certain cultural issue (such as the prison), and that issue's political implications.

The originality of Foucault's analysis of the links between the individually constituted person and the social whole continues to provide inspiration for sociology. That academic branch is constantly concerned with a basic epistemological* debate about structure versus agency. And although Foucault's original frame of reference is the West, his theories have been applied in studies of other parts of the world, demonstrating, for example, how illnesses may be linked to discursive regimes—roughly, how we talk about illness—rather than to physical issues.[17]

Finally, Foucault's study of power benefits from its timelessness. *Discipline and Punish* is not an open attack on the exercise of power by any specific group or institution. It is a study of techniques that come into play in relationships between individuals, incorporated by those individuals and embodied in the structure of social interactions. As long as human beings live alongside each other, these issues will remain relevant.

NOTES

1 Michel Foucault, Discipline and Punish: The Birth of the Prison (Sheridan, NY: Vintage Books, 1979), 200.

2 Michael Hardt and Antonio Negri, *Empire* (Cambridge, MA: Harvard University Press, 2009): 22.

3 Colin Wilson, "Michel Foucault: Friend or Foe of the Left?" *International Socialism*, March 31, 2008.

4 David M. Berry. *Critical Theory and the Digital* (New York: Bloomsbury: 2014).

5 Cynthia Weber, *International Relations Theory: A Critical Introduction*, 4th edn. (New York: Routledge, 2014). See especially: 88, 140, 149, 231.

6 Ian Marsh and Gaynor Melville, *Crime, Justice and the Media* (New York: Routledge, 2014 [2009]).

7 David Lyon, Theorizing Surveillance (New York: Routledge, 2011 [2006]).

8 David Armstrong, "The Subject and the Social in Medicine: An Appreciation of Michel Foucault," *Sociology of Health & Illness* 7, no. 1 (1985): 111.

9 Armstrong, "Subject and the Social"; David Armstrong, "Foucault and the Sociology of Health and Illness," in *Foucault, Health and Medicine*, ed. Alan Petersen and Robin Bunton (London and New York: Routledge, 1997).

10 David Armstrong, "Public Health Spaces and the Fabrication of Identity," *Sociology* 27, no. 3 (August 1993): 393–410.

11 David Armstrong, *Political Anatomy of the Body: Medical Knowledge in Britain in the Twentieth Century* (Cambridge: Cambridge University Press, 1983).

12 Nikolas Rose*, Governing the Soul: The Shaping of the Private Self* (Florence, KY: Taylor & Francis/Routledge, 1990).

13 Foucault, *Discipline and Punish*, 27.

14 William Ray Arney and Jane Neill, "The Location of Pain in Childbirth: Natural Childbirth and the Transformation of Obstetrics," *Sociology of Health & Illness* 4, no. 1 (1982): 1–24.

15 Deborah Lupton, *The Imperative of Health: Public Health and the Regulated Body* (London; Thousand Oaks, CA: Sage Publications, 1995).

16 Foucault, *Discipline and Punish*, 27.

17 See: Stefan Ecks, "Pharmaceutical Citizenship: Antidepressant Marketing and the Promise of Demarginalization in India," *Anthropology & Medicine* 12, no. 3 (2005): 239–54.

GLOSSARY

GLOSSARY OF TERMS

Administrative science: the study of governance, management, or public administration, including the study of policies, how policies are implemented, and how administrative systems are managed.

Algerian War (1954–62): a war between various anti-colonialist factions of the French colony of Algeria and France. The anti-colonialists wanted to attain independence from French rule. The war occurred on both French and Algerian soil and resulted in several hundred thousand casualties, most of whom were Algerian. It is among the most violent wars in both Algerian and French history, and remains a traumatic memory for both countries.

Anthropology: the study of human beings and human behavior, and their cultures. The discipline draws on a number of other fields in the physical, biological, and social sciences, and humanities.

Anti-psychiatry: opposition to conventional psychiatric methods and treatments. Although this stance has been around for two centuries, it gained momentum in the 1960s, when political activists and scholars began to question standard definitions of mental illness, and to query how these were developed.

Archaeology: the analysis of artifacts and ruins to understand past human activity and the societies from which they came. Foucault used the term in the first half of his career to refer to his approach to historical research: examining traces of past discourses and systems provides a way to understand the processes that have brought us to where we are today.

Bretton Woods: a system of monetary management that regulated commercial and financial relationships among the major industrial economies of the mid-twentieth century

Carceral: of or relating to jails, prisons, and similar institutions.

Carceral continuum: a term Foucault uses to define modern society's reliance on disciplinary and punitive practices. Not only prisons and reformatories, but schools, factories, offices, and hospitals use carceral methods to enforce their systems. The term "continuum" refers to the differing gradations of punishment that these various institutions inflict on their subjects, all in a bid to create conformity. The continuum's greatest achievement is to have legitimized the power to punish: we take it for granted that teachers, doctors, and employers are there to judge us.

CCTV (closed-circuit television): a term used to refer to the use of television cameras to monitor public or private places. It is commonly used in places such as banks, shops, and airports where institutions or governments have an interest in observing the behavior of individuals.

Coercion: the act of manipulating someone to do something against his or her will.

Colonialism: the establishment and maintenance of a colony in a territory by a foreign and dominant power. During the European colonial period, lasting from the sixteenth to the twentieth century, European powers established extensive colonies in Asia, Africa, and the Americas, with far-reaching implications.

Communicative rationality: a term coined by the influential sociologist Jürgen Habermas to refer to the theory that rationality is a product of successful communication between individuals.

Contingency: a philosophical term used to denote that a particular proposition is not universally or always true, but rather that its truth depends on other factors. When Foucault refers to something as being historically contingent, for example, he means that its occurrence was due to a particular historical context, but also that it could have occurred differently, or not at all.

Criminology: the study of the causes, nature, definition, and prevention of crime and deviance at both an individual and a societal level.

Cultural studies: an academic field that examines cultural phenomena such as class structure, ideology, national formations, gender, sexuality, and perceptions of ethnicity through a number of different theoretical approaches, including anthropology, political science, and sociology. Such study is premised on the assumption that culture is not fixed, but rather is a constantly evolving process susceptible to and reflective of broader socioeconomic, political, and historical changes.

Cyberveillance: the monitoring of an individual or a group's computer or Internet activity, using hardware or software, which may be undertaken by a range of entities, including employers, corporations, and the government.

Dehumanization: the systematic process of demonizing another person or persons by making them appear less than human, and therefore not deserving of humane treatment. Dehumanization is central to contexts such as war, as it enables one to justify killing, and to systems such as colonialism, as it vindicates the curtailing of human rights and of enforcing that curtailment with violence.

Digital culture/digital culture studies: new media and new media devices in contemporary culture and the study of them.

Discipline: as it appears in *Discipline and Punish*, a mechanism by which power is exerted. It is not power itself. Rather, it refers to various ways in which individuals are encouraged to self-regulate, such as the use of timetables, the organization of space, and drills to encourage certain forms of bodily comportment.

Discourse/Discursive practice/discursive regime: in Foucault's use, a way of speaking that is a product of history and power. Discursive practices are the set of rules that inform the ways of speaking available to the individual in a given time and place. The term "discursive regime" refers to the overlaying of power with ways of speaking such that only certain things can be said and certain things are unsayable.

Econometric: relating to, or characterized by the application of statistical theory or methods to economic data.

Economics: an academic field in the social sciences that examines economic systems, structures, policies, and trends and their influence on the production, distribution, and consumption of goods and services.

Emancipation: the procurement of social, economic, and/or political rights or equality by a previously disenfranchised group.

Enlightenment: also known as the Age of Reason, the era roughly between 1650 and 1780 when Western European culture and thought progressively came to privilege individualism, reason, and analysis over religious faith. The period was characterized by the view that rational thought could conquer any ambiguity and that logic could solve the world's mysteries.

Epistemology: a branch of philosophy concerned with the nature of knowledge, which seeks to understand how we "know" what we know.

Existentialism: a branch of philosophy that holds that the individual—as opposed to society, the state, or religion—is the foundation of meaning, order, and morals.

Feminism: series of ideologies and movements concerned with equal social, political, cultural, and economic rights for women, including equal rights in the home, workplace, education, and government.

Genealogy: in literal terms, the study of family lineages and histories. Foucault however uses the term to refer to his historical approach from *Discipline and Punish* onward. He distinguishes it from his previous "archaeological" approach, arguing that although both methods address the history of knowledge systems and discourses, genealogy traces the role that power has played in those systems, and in defining certain things as "true" and others as "false."

Globalization: a process of integration and interaction among the governments, peoples, and companies of different countries. The process is fueled by international trade and investment, and propelled by information technology.

Governmentality: term used by Foucault in *Discipline and Punish* and his last work, *History of Sexuality* to define two things: a particular form of administrating populations in modern Europe following the emergence of the nation state and, later, all of the systems and mechanisms used to govern populations and individuals, including forms of self-governance.

History: an academic field dedicated to the study and interpretation of past events and their meaning, including the study of the discrepancies between different cultures' and different generations' understanding of the same event.

Humanism: a branch of philosophy that tends to emphasize the importance of a universal humanity and human nature, instead of society or religion, as the font of meaning and morality.

Human resource management: a branch or department of a company that oversees the discipline and business functioning of its employees (who are known as human resources since they contribute to the output of the company). This department oversees the skills and qualifications of the company's workforce, and arranges salaries, benefits, and time off.

International relations (IR): the study of international systems of governance. IR scholars might study the relationships between actors such as states, international organizations, non-governmental organizations (NGOs), and multinational corporations.

Iranian Revolution (1979): also known as the 1979 Revolution or the Islamic Revolution, the culmination of various uprisings aimed at overthrowing the country's oppressive monarchy, which was viewed by many as a puppet of the West and as overly influenced by Western values. The events began in 1977 at the instigation of the Iranian left and several student movements, and eventually led to the establishment of the Iranian Republic, which looked to distance itself from both the capitalist values of the West and the communist values of the USSR. Foucault was an avid supporter of the Revolution.

Literary studies/criticism: the evaluation, study, and interpretation of literature.

Marxism: a cultural, philosophical, socioeconomic, political, and aesthetic movement based on the work of the nineteenth-century political economist Karl Marx. Marxist theorists and writers are concerned with the growth of social inequality under capitalism, and the influence this has on culture and society.

Materialism: a school of thought that holds that physical matter is the key shaper of society and of historical trends. For example, Karl Marx held that the key catalysts of social change are the changes in the ways people provide for themselves materially.

Media studies: an academic field that examines the content, cultural effects, and history of new media, and particularly mass media such as television, radio, and cinema. The field combines the approaches of literary criticism and art history (in its analysis of particular forms of media and their content) with those of sociology, political science, and history (in its examination of the sociocultural conditions that gave rise to particular forms of media, and the effects, in turn, that those forms have had on content).

Modernity: a term used in the humanities and the social sciences to refer to a period of time, generally understood to stretch from the sixteenth to early twentieth century, marked by a rejection of traditional values.

Neoliberalism: set of economic policies that encourages economic liberalization, free trade, open markets, privatization, deregulation, and the enhancement of the role of the private sector.

Normalization: in sociology, term used to refer to the processes by which particular ideas of modes of behavior become common practice. However, Foucault uses the term in relation to institutional power's influence on creating conformity: that is, how disciplinary regimes create conformity among citizens and eradicate eccentricity or errant behavior. The strength of modern disciplinary powers lies in their capacity to exert social control efficiently (expending minimal resources), making people fall into line and follow the rules.

NSA (National Security Agency): an American governmental agency responsible for the monitoring of information and individuals that may have implications for US national security interests. In 2013, the US whistleblower Edward Snowden controversially released information detailing the extent of the NSA's secret surveillance practices.

Organizational sociology: branch of sociology that looks at the inner functions of modern organizations, and their broader social role. This might include how institutions divide labor, allocate resources, or respond to change.

Panopticism: theory that the model of the prison, as encapsulated by the Panopticon and its capacity to make individuals self-regulate, is a model for all power relations in society.

Panopticon: a concept for a prison advanced by the British social reformer Jeremy Bentham. The structure was designed to permit invisible observation of a large number of inmates by a single prison guard. The belief that they were being watched would lead prisoners to regulate their behavior and effectively govern themselves, making the guard's presence obsolete.

Paris Riots of 1968: a period of civil unrest marked by strikes by workers, demonstrations, and the occupation of university buildings by students.

Penology: a branch of criminology that studies the theory and practice of punishment and penal institutions, and their effectiveness.

Phenomenology: in philosophy, the study of the structures that inform our experience and our consciousness. In psychology, it is the study of subjective experience.

Philosophy: a field of the humanities that studies fundamental human problems related to reality, knowledge, existence, reason, language, and values.

Political science: a field of the social sciences that examines government policies and politics, and the dynamics of nation, government, and state.

Poststructuralism: a field of philosophy that emerged in the 1970s as a response to the perceived rigidity and a historicism of structuralism. Scholars in the field argued that structuralism did not account for the instability of knowledge itself: the very structure of knowledge is a social construct, which means that we can never fully escape the systems we are looking to understand. Poststructuralists argue that all forms of knowledge are contingent upon certain assumptions about what constitutes the truth. In turn, this means that any interpretation of a text, historical event, or idea can be disproven the moment the tenets on which it is premised are called into question. Although Foucault resisted being defined as a poststructuralist, many of his ideas can be seen to fall within this purview.

Power-knowledge: a term coined by Foucault to denote that knowledge is always constituted by power and power by knowledge; in other words, to "know" someone—to classify them—is to have power over them.

Psychiatry: a branch of medicine that deals with the study, treatment, and prevention of mental, emotional, or behavioral disorders.

Psychology: an academic and applied discipline concerning the study and treatment of mental behavior and mental functions.

Queer theory: a broad field of poststructuralist theory associated with both LGBT (lesbian, gay, bisexual, transgender) studies and women's studies, concerned with inquiry into both what is considered "normal" and supposedly deviant identity categories.

Rationality: the state of being reasonable—that is, to believe and to act according to one's reasons for believing, and one's reasons for action. Rational thought—thought based on reason and logic—has been the subject of inquiry among sociologists and philosophers since the Enlightenment.

Le regard **(the gaze**): a term used by Foucault to describe the role of visibility in modern systems of knowledge and power. Institutional surveillance—be it by the state, a school administration, hospital staff, prison warden, or company head—enables the normalization of a system's subjects—which is to say, it enforces people within that system to conform to its standards, both in terms of obeying its laws and in acting and thinking the way the system wants. Foucault argues that *le regard* modifies individuals themselves: under institutional surveillance, we become the sum of what we abstain from doing for fear of being seen, judged, or punished.

Sociology: the academic study of social behavior. The discipline examines the origins and development of social relations, their different modes of organization, and different social institutions.

Sociology of law: a branch of sociology that looks at the creation and implementation of laws from a theoretical and empirical perspective, and at the role of legal institutions in mediating social relations. Some scholars see it as a subdiscipline of legal studies, or, alternately, as a field that combines elements of sociology and law.

Sociology of punishment: a branch of sociology that deals specifically with why and how we punish, including the reasons underlying punishment and the implementation of particular forms of punishment and their effects.

Structuralism: a school of philosophical and sociological thought that gained sway in the 1950s and 1960s partly as a counter to existential humanism. Its main proponents were the anthropologist Claude Lévi-Strauss and the psychoanalyst Jacques Lacan. These scholars argued that human experience, culture, and knowledge are contingent upon larger, underlying ideological, sociocultural, and economic structures: our perception of ourselves, and our understanding of the world, is shaped by specific social constructs. At the time it emerged, it was often viewed as a direct opponent of Marxism. Foucault has been associated with structuralism, but he resisted this classification.

Subjugation: conquering and gaining control of someone or something and rendering them subordinate.

Surveillance: monitoring of behavior, usually in order to control, modify, or manipulate it.

Totalitarianism: a system of government in which the state has complete control over every aspect of society. Nazi Germany and Soviet Russia are examples of totalitarian states.

Vietnam War (1955–75): also known as the Second Indochina War, a conflict fought in Laos, Cambodia, and Vietnam between North Vietnam and South Vietnam. It is referred to as a Cold War-era conflict due to the role played by competing global powers: North Vietnam was supported by the Soviet Union, China, and other communist countries, while South Vietnam was supported by the United States and other anti-communist countries including France. The North Vietnamese saw the conflict as essentially a colonial one, and argued that the United States and France's role in South Vietnam rendered it a puppet state.

Welfare state: a system of social or governmental organization that incorporates the provision of support and promotion of well-being for citizens. Examples of social welfare include public education and universal health care.

PEOPLE MENTIONED IN THE TEXT

C. Fred Alford (b. 1947) is a political psychologist who wrote a seminal article critiquing Foucault's account of the workings of prison life.

Louis Althusser (1918–90) was a French Marxist philosopher who is often associated today with the school of structuralism. However, Althusser was critical of certain aspects of structuralist thought, and spent his life supporting the central tenets of Marxism.

Zygmunt Bauman (b. 1925) is a Polish sociologist and one of the world's foremost social thinkers. He has written widely on subjects as diffuse as the Holocaust, rationality, modernity, and consumerism. He is currently professor emeritus of sociology at the University of Leeds.

Simone de Beauvoir (1908–86) is perhaps the most famous, and influential, feminist philosopher and writer of the twentieth century. She is best known for her writings on feminist existentialism and feminist theory, as well as for her lifelong relationship with Jean-Paul Sartre.

Jeremy Bentham (1748–1832) was a British social reformer who became well-known for his contributions to philosophies of law, his advocacy for the abolition of slavery and the death penalty, and his strong opinions regarding the separation of church and state. His design of the Panopticon prison building, although never realized, had a great influence on later generations of thinkers, including Foucault.

Emile Durkheim (1858–1917) was a French sociologist and philosopher. He is also generally recognized as the founder of sociology. Durkheim's work was largely concerned with societies' transition into "modernity"—an era characterized by the waning power of the church, new developments in technology, and the growth of cities. He is best known for his study of societal organization, *The Division of Labor in Society* (1893), and his writings on crime.

Nancy Fraser (b. 1947) is a political philosopher recognized for her extensive writings on the concept of "justice." She is well-known for being one of the earliest English-speaking academics to do extensive work on Foucauldian thinking.

Jürgen Habermas (b. 1929) is a highly regarded social scientist and philosopher. He and Foucault clashed over the quality and emancipatory potential of reason. Habermas has been the strongest defender writing contemporarily of the Enlightenment's faith in reason, standing in stark contrast to Foucault's critique of reason as culturally produced and contingent.

Michael Hardt (b. 1960) is an American political philosopher and literary theorist known for his collaborations with Antonio Negri on *Empire* (2000) and *Multitude* (2004).

Georg Wilhelm Friedrich Hegel (1770–1831) was a German philosopher and a major figure in the idealism movement. He became well known for his historicist and realist accounts of reality. His concept of a "system" of integration between mind and nature, subject and object, etc., was one of the first conceptual moves that acknowledged contradictions and oppositions within such a system.

Jean Hyppolite (1907–68) was a French philosopher and follower of Georg Hegel and the German philosophical movement, and a prominent figure in French thinking in the mid-twentieth century.

Foucault studied under him and was profoundly shaped by his ideas on the relationship between history and philosophy.

Karl Marx (1818–83) was a German political philosopher and economist whose analysis of class relations under capitalism and articulation of a more egalitarian system provided the basis for communism. Together with Friedrich Engels, Marx wrote *The Communist Manifesto* (1848). He articulated his full theory of production and class relations in *Das Kapital* (1867–94).

Maurice Merleau-Ponty (1908–61) was a French phenomenological philosopher and writer, and the only major philosopher of his time to incorporate descriptive psychology in his work. This influenced later phenomenologists, who went on to use cognitive science and psychology in their studies.

Antonio Negri (b. 1933) is a prominent Italian Marxist political philosopher and activist. He is most widely known for his collaborations with Michael Hardt on *Empire* (2000) and *Multitude* (2004).

Friedrich Nietzsche (1844–1900) was a radical German philosopher, philologist, poet, and cultural critic whose writings had a profound influence on Western philosophy. He is best known for his views on the "death of God," his writings on morality, and his questioning of the objectivity of truth.

Nikolas Rose (b. 1947) is an influential British social theorist and sociologist who has written on mental health policy and risk, the sociology and history of psychiatry, and the social implications of new psychopharmacological developments in the area of mental health. He is best known for his writings on Foucault and for reviving interest in Foucault's concept of governmentality in the Anglophone world.

Jean-Paul Sartre (1905–80) was a French existential philosopher, and a leading thinker in the schools of twentieth-century French philosophy and Marxism. His work, including novels and plays, relied heavily on the idea that individuals are "condemned to be free," and that there is no creator.

Edward Snowden (b. 1983) is an American computer professional known for leaking classified information gathered by the United States National Security Agency (NSA) to the public beginning in June 2013. Snowden's leaks revealed various global surveillance mechanisms operating between the US and other countries in conjunction with several global telecommunications companies, fueling debates about national security versus individual privacy.

Barbara Townley (b. 1954) is a sociologist and social theorist known for her work on Foucault as well as for her writings in management studies, including the use of performance reviews in higher education, government, and cultural industries.

WORKS CITED

WORKS CITED

Alford, C. Fred. "What Would It Matter if Everything Foucault Said About Prison Were Wrong? *Discipline and Punish* After Twenty Years." *Theory and Society* 29, no. 1 (2000): 125–46. Accessed August 9, 2015. doi:10.1023/A:1007014831641.

Armstrong, David. "Foucault and the Sociology of Health and Illness." In *Foucault, Health and Medicine*, edited by Alan Petersen and Robin Bunyon. London and New York: Routledge, 1997.

————. *Political Anatomy of the Body: Medical Knowledge in Britain in the Twentieth Century*. Cambridge: Cambridge University Press, 1983.

————. "Public Health Spaces and the Fabrication of Identity." *Sociology* 27, no. 3 (August 1993): 393–410. Accessed August 9, 2015. doi:10.1177/0038 038593027003004.

————. "The Subject and the Social in Medicine: An Appreciation of Michel Foucault." *Sociology of Health & Illness* 7, no. 1 (1985): 108–117. Accessed August 9, 2015. doi:10.1111/1467–9566.ep10831391.

Arney, William Ray, and Jane Neill. "The Location of Pain in Childbirth: Natural Childbirth and the Transformation of Obstetrics." *Sociology of Health & Illness* 4, no. 1 (1982): 1–24.

Ashenden, Samantha, and David Owen. *Foucault Contra Habermas: Recasting the Dialogue Between Genealogy and Critical Theory*. Thousand Oaks, Calif.; London: SAGE, 1999.

Bauman, Zygmunt. "On Postmodern Uses of Sex." *Theory, Culture & Society* 15, no. 3 (1998).

Berry, David M. *Critical Theory and the Digital*. New York: Bloomsbury: 2014.

Braithwaite, John. "What's Wrong with the Sociology of Punishment?" *Theoretical Criminology* 7, no. 1 (February 2003): 5–28. Accessed August 9, 2015. doi:10.1177/1362480603007001198.

Burchell, Graham, Colin Gordon, and Peter Miller, eds. *The Foucault Effect: Studies in Governmentality*. Chicago, IL: University of Chicago Press, 1991.

Burrell, Gibson. "Modernism, Post Modernism and Organizational Analysis 2: The Contribution of Michel Foucault." *Organization Studies* 9, no. 2 (April 1988): 221–35. Accessed August 9, 2015. doi:10.1177/017084068800900205.

Chomsky, Noam, and Michel Foucault. *The Chomsky–Foucault Debate*. New York, NY: The New Press, 2006.

Durkheim, Emile, and Lewis A. Coser. *The Division of Labor in Society*. New York, NY: Free Press, 1997.

Ecks, Stefan. "Pharmaceutical Citizenship: Antidepressant Marketing and the Promise of Demarginalization in India." *Anthropology & Medicine* 12, no. 3 (2005): 239–54. Accessed August 9, 2015. doi:10.1080/13648470500291360.

Eribon, Dider. *Michel Foucault et ses contemporains*. Paris: Fayard, 1994.

Faubion, James D. "Toward an Anthropology of Ethics: Foucault and the Pedagogies of Autopoiesis." *Representations* 74, no. 1 (Spring 2001): 83–104.

Ferguson, James. *The Anti-politics Machine: Development, Depoliticization, and Bureaucratic Power in Lesotho*. Minneapolis: University of Minnesota Press, 1994.

Foucault, Michel. *Discipline and Punish: The Birth of the Prison*. Sheridan, NY: Vintage Books, 1979.

————. "Governmentality." In *The Essential Foucault*, edited by Paul Rabinow and Nikolas Rose. New York and London: The New Press, 2003.

————. *Power/Knowledge: Selected Interviews and Other Writings, 1972–1977*. New York: Random House Digital, 1980.

————. *Security, Territory, Population: Lectures at the Collège de France, 1977–1978*. London and New York: Palgrave MacMillan, 2007.

————. "What Is Enlightenment?" In *The Foucault Effect: Studies in Governmentality*, edited by Graham Burchell, Colin Gordon, and Peter Miller. Chicago, IL: University of Chicago Press, 1991.

Nancy Fraser. "From Discipline to Flexibilization? Rereading Foucault in the Shadow of Globalization." *Constellations* 10, no. 2 (2003): 160–71.

Garland, David. "Foucault's *Discipline and Punish*—An Exposition and Critique." *Law & Social Inquiry* 11, no. 4 (1986): 847–80. Accessed August 10, 2015. doi:10.1111/j.1747–4469.1986.tb00270.x.

————. "Frameworks of Inquiry in the Sociology of Punishment." *The British Journal of Sociology* 41, no. 1 (March 1990).

Guthman, Julie, and Melanie DuPuis. "Embodying Neoliberalism: Economy, Culture, and the Politics of Fat." *Environment and Planning D: Society and Space* 24, no. 3 (2006): 427–48. Accessed August 10, 2015. doi:10.1068/d3904.

Halperin, David. *Saint Foucault: Towards a Gay Hagiography*. Oxford and New York: Oxford University Press, 1997.

Hardt, Michael, and Antonio Negri. *Empire.* Cambridge, MA: Harvard University Press, 2009.

Hekman, Susan, ed. *Feminist Interpretations of Michel Foucault*. University Park, PA: Pennsylvania State University Press, 1996.

Hunt, Alan, and Gary Wickham. *Foucault and Law: Towards a Sociology of Law as Governance*. Boulder, CO.; London: Pluto Press, 1994.

Jessop, Bob. "From Micro-powers to Governmentality: Foucault's Work on Statehood, State Formation, Statecraft and State Power." *Political Geography* 26, no. 1 (January 2007): 34–40. Accessed August 10, 2015. doi:10.1016/j. polgeo.2006.08.002.

Kelly, Michael, Michel Foucault, and Jürgen Habermas. *Critique and Power: Recasting the Foucault/Habermas Debate*. Cambridge, Mass.; London: MIT Press, 1994.

Larmour, David H. J., Paul Allen Miller, and Charles Platter. *Rethinking Sexuality: Foucault and Classical Antiquity*. Princeton, NJ: Princeton University Press, 1997.

Lemke, Thomas. "An Indigestible Meal? Foucault, Governmentality and State Theory." *Distinktion: Scandinavian Journal of Social Theory* 8, no. 2 (2007): 43–64. Accessed August 10, 2015. doi:10.1080/1600910X.2007.9672946.

— — —. "'The Birth of Bio-politics': Michel Foucault's Lecture at the Collège De France on Neo-liberal Governmentality." *Economy and Society* 30, no. 2 (2001). Accessed August 10, 2015. doi:10.1080/03085140120042271.

Lupton, Deborah. *The Imperative of Health: Public Health and the Regulated Body*. London; Thousand Oaks, CA: Sage Publications, 1995.

David Lyon. *Theorizing Surveillance*. New York: Routledge, 2011 [2006].

Marsh, Ian, and Gaynor Melville. *Crime, Justice and the Media*. New York: Routledge, 2014 [2009].

Mathiesen, Thomas. "The Viewer Society: Foucault's Panopticon Revisited." *Theoretical Criminology* 1, no. 2 (1997).

Miller, James. *The Passion of Michel Foucault*. Cambridge, MA: Harvard University Press, 1993.

Nietzsche, Friedrich Wilhelm. *The Genealogy of Morals*. London and New York: Macmillan, 1897.

Rose, Nikolas. *Governing the Soul: The Shaping of the Private Self*. Florence, KY: Taylor & Francis/Routledge, 1990.

— — —. *Powers of Freedom: Reframing Political Thought*. Cambridge: Cambridge University Press, 1999.

Rupp, Jan C. "Michel Foucault, Body Politics and the Rise and Expansion of Modern Anatomy." *Journal of Historical Sociology* 5, no. 1 (1992): 31–60. Accessed August 10, 2015. doi:10.1111/j.1467–6443.1992.tb00022.x.

Savelsberg, Joachim J. "Knowledge, Domination, and Criminal Punishment." *American Journal of Sociology* 99, no. 4 (January 1994): 911–43.

Sawicki, Jana. *Disciplining Foucault: Feminism, Power, and the Body*. London: Routledge, 1991.

Townley, Barbara. "Foucault, Power/Knowledge, and Its Relevance for Human Resource Management." *The Academy of Management Review* 18, no. 3 (July 1993): 518–45.

Weber, Cynthia. *International Relations Theory: A Critical Introduction*, 4th edition. New York: Routledge, 2014.

Wilson, Colin. "Michel Foucault: Friend or Foe of the Left?" *International Socialism*, March 31, 2008.

Zamindar, Vazira Fazila-Yacoobali. *The Long Partition and the Making of Modern South Asia: Refugees, Boundaries, Histories*. New York, NY; Chichester: Columbia University Press, 2007.

THE MACAT LIBRARY
BY DISCIPLINE

The Macat Library By Discipline

AFRICANA STUDIES

Chinua Achebe's *An Image of Africa: Racism in Conrad's Heart of Darkness*
W. E. B. Du Bois's *The Souls of Black Folk*
Zora Neale Huston's *Characteristics of Negro Expression*
Martin Luther King Jr's *Why We Can't Wait*
Toni Morrison's *Playing in the Dark: Whiteness in the American Literary Imagination*

ANTHROPOLOGY

Arjun Appadurai's *Modernity at Large: Cultural Dimensions of Globalisation*
Philippe Ariès's *Centuries of Childhood*
Franz Boas's *Race, Language and Culture*
Kim Chan & Renée Mauborgne's *Blue Ocean Strategy*
Jared Diamond's *Guns, Germs & Steel: the Fate of Human Societies*
Jared Diamond's *Collapse: How Societies Choose to Fail or Survive*
E. E. Evans-Pritchard's *Witchcraft, Oracles and Magic Among the Azande*
James Ferguson's *The Anti-Politics Machine*
Clifford Geertz's *The Interpretation of Cultures*
David Graeber's *Debt: the First 5000 Years*
Karen Ho's *Liquidated: An Ethnography of Wall Street*
Geert Hofstede's *Culture's Consequences: Comparing Values, Behaviors, Institutes and Organizations across Nations*
Claude Lévi-Strauss's *Structural Anthropology*
Jay Macleod's *Ain't No Makin' It: Aspirations and Attainment in a Low-Income Neighborhood*
Saba Mahmood's *The Politics of Piety: The Islamic Revival and the Feminist Subjec*t
Marcel Mauss's *The Gift*

BUSINESS

Jean Lave & Etienne Wenger's *Situated Learning*
Theodore Levitt's *Marketing Myopia*
Burton G. Malkiel's *A Random Walk Down Wall Street*
Douglas McGregor's *The Human Side of Enterprise*
Michael Porter's *Competitive Strategy: Creating and Sustaining Superior Performance*
John Kotter's *Leading Change*
C. K. Prahalad & Gary Hamel's *The Core Competence of the Corporation*

CRIMINOLOGY

Michelle Alexander's *The New Jim Crow: Mass Incarceration in the Age of Colorblindness*
Michael R. Gottfredson & Travis Hirschi's *A General Theory of Crime*
Richard Herrnstein & Charles A. Murray's *The Bell Curve: Intelligence and Class Structure in American Life*
Elizabeth Loftus's *Eyewitness Testimony*
Jay Macleod's *Ain't No Makin' It: Aspirations and Attainment in a Low-Income Neighborhood*
Philip Zimbardo's *The Lucifer Effect*

ECONOMICS

Janet Abu-Lughod's *Before European Hegemony*
Ha-Joon Chang's *Kicking Away the Ladder*
David Brion Davis's *The Problem of Slavery in the Age of Revolution*
Milton Friedman's *The Role of Monetary Policy*
Milton Friedman's *Capitalism and Freedom*
David Graeber's *Debt: the First 5000 Years*
Friedrich Hayek's *The Road to Serfdom*
Karen Ho's *Liquidated: An Ethnography of Wall Street*

John Maynard Keynes's *The General Theory of Employment, Interest and Money*
Charles P. Kindleberger's *Manias, Panics and Crashes*
Robert Lucas's *Why Doesn't Capital Flow from Rich to Poor Countries?*
Burton G. Malkiel's *A Random Walk Down Wall Street*
Thomas Robert Malthus's *An Essay on the Principle of Population*
Karl Marx's *Capital*
Thomas Piketty's *Capital in the Twenty-First Century*
Amartya Sen's *Development as Freedom*
Adam Smith's *The Wealth of Nations*
Nassim Nicholas Taleb's *The Black Swan: The Impact of the Highly Improbable*
Amos Tversky's & Daniel Kahneman's *Judgment under Uncertainty: Heuristics and Biases*
Mahbub Ul Haq's *Reflections on Human Development*
Max Weber's *The Protestant Ethic and the Spirit of Capitalism*

FEMINISM AND GENDER STUDIES

Judith Butler's *Gender Trouble*
Simone De Beauvoir's *The Second Sex*
Michel Foucault's *History of Sexuality*
Betty Friedan's *The Feminine Mystique*
Saba Mahmood's *The Politics of Piety: The Islamic Revival and the Feminist Subjec*t
Joan Wallach Scott's *Gender and the Politics of History*
Mary Wollstonecraft's *A Vindication of the Rights of Woman*
Virginia Woolf's *A Room of One's Own*

GEOGRAPHY

The Brundtland Report's *Our Common Future*
Rachel Carson's *Silent Spring*
Charles Darwin's *On the Origin of Species*
James Ferguson's *The Anti-Politics Machine*
Jane Jacobs's *The Death and Life of Great American Cities*
James Lovelock's *Gaia: A New Look at Life on Earth*
Amartya Sen's *Development as Freedom*
Mathis Wackernagel & William Rees's *Our Ecological Footprint*

HISTORY

Janet Abu-Lughod's *Before European Hegemony*
Benedict Anderson's *Imagined Communities*
Bernard Bailyn's *The Ideological Origins of the American Revolution*
Hanna Batatu's *The Old Social Classes And The Revolutionary Movements Of Iraq*
Christopher Browning's *Ordinary Men: Reserve Police Batallion 101 and the Final Solution in Poland*
Edmund Burke's *Reflections on the Revolution in France*
William Cronon's *Nature's Metropolis: Chicago And The Great West*
Alfred W. Crosby's *The Columbian Exchange*
Hamid Dabashi's *Iran: A People Interrupted*
David Brion Davis's *The Problem of Slavery in the Age of Revolution*
Nathalie Zemon Davis's *The Return of Martin Guerre*
Jared Diamond's *Guns, Germs & Steel: the Fate of Human Societies*
Frank Dikotter's *Mao's Great Famine*
John W Dower's *War Without Mercy: Race And Power In The Pacific War*
W. E. B. Du Bois's *The Souls of Black Folk*
Richard J. Evans's *In Defence of History*
Lucien Febvre's *The Problem of Unbelief in the 16th Century*
Sheila Fitzpatrick's *Everyday Stalinism*

The Macat Library By Discipline

Eric Foner's *Reconstruction: America's Unfinished Revolution, 1863-1877*
Michel Foucault's *Discipline and Punish*
Michel Foucault's *History of Sexuality*
Francis Fukuyama's *The End of History and the Last Man*
John Lewis Gaddis's *We Now Know: Rethinking Cold War History*
Ernest Gellner's *Nations and Nationalism*
Eugene Genovese's *Roll, Jordan, Roll: The World the Slaves Made*
Carlo Ginzburg's *The Night Battles*
Daniel Goldhagen's *Hitler's Willing Executioners*
Jack Goldstone's *Revolution and Rebellion in the Early Modern World*
Antonio Gramsci's *The Prison Notebooks*
Alexander Hamilton, John Jay & James Madison's *The Federalist Papers*
Christopher Hill's *The World Turned Upside Down*
Carole Hillenbrand's *The Crusades: Islamic Perspectives*
Thomas Hobbes's *Leviathan*
Eric Hobsbawm's *The Age Of Revolution*
John A. Hobson's *Imperialism: A Study*
Albert Hourani's *History of the Arab Peoples*
Samuel P. Huntington's *The Clash of Civilizations and the Remaking of World Order*
C. L. R. James's *The Black Jacobins*
Tony Judt's *Postwar: A History of Europe Since 1945*
Ernst Kantorowicz's *The King's Two Bodies: A Study in Medieval Political Theology*
Paul Kennedy's *The Rise and Fall of the Great Powers*
Ian Kershaw's *The "Hitler Myth": Image and Reality in the Third Reich*
John Maynard Keynes's *The General Theory of Employment, Interest and Money*
Charles P. Kindleberger's *Manias, Panics and Crashes*
Martin Luther King Jr's *Why We Can't Wait*
Henry Kissinger's *World Order: Reflections on the Character of Nations and the Course of History*
Thomas Kuhn's *The Structure of Scientific Revolutions*
Georges Lefebvre's *The Coming of the French Revolution*
John Locke's *Two Treatises of Government*
Niccolò Machiavelli's *The Prince*
Thomas Robert Malthus's *An Essay on the Principle of Population*
Mahmood Mamdani's *Citizen and Subject: Contemporary Africa And The Legacy Of Late Colonialism*
Karl Marx's *Capital*
Stanley Milgram's *Obedience to Authority*
John Stuart Mill's *On Liberty*
Thomas Paine's *Common Sense*
Thomas Paine's *Rights of Man*
Geoffrey Parker's *Global Crisis: War, Climate Change and Catastrophe in the Seventeenth Century*
Jonathan Riley-Smith's *The First Crusade and the Idea of Crusading*
Jean-Jacques Rousseau's *The Social Contract*
Joan Wallach Scott's *Gender and the Politics of History*
Theda Skocpol's *States and Social Revolutions*
Adam Smith's *The Wealth of Nations*
Timothy Snyder's *Bloodlands: Europe Between Hitler and Stalin*
Sun Tzu's *The Art of War*
Keith Thomas's *Religion and the Decline of Magic*
Thucydides's *The History of the Peloponnesian War*
Frederick Jackson Turner's *The Significance of the Frontier in American History*
Odd Arne Westad's *The Global Cold War: Third World Interventions And The Making Of Our Times*

LITERATURE

Chinua Achebe's *An Image of Africa: Racism in Conrad's Heart of Darkness*
Roland Barthes's *Mythologies*
Homi K. Bhabha's *The Location of Culture*
Judith Butler's *Gender Trouble*
Simone De Beauvoir's *The Second Sex*
Ferdinand De Saussure's *Course in General Linguistics*
T. S. Eliot's *The Sacred Wood: Essays on Poetry and Criticism*
Zora Neale Huston's *Characteristics of Negro Expression*
Toni Morrison's *Playing in the Dark: Whiteness in the American Literary Imagination*
Edward Said's *Orientalism*
Gayatri Chakravorty Spivak's *Can the Subaltern Speak?*
Mary Wollstonecraft's *A Vindication of the Rights of Women*
Virginia Woolf's *A Room of One's Own*

PHILOSOPHY

Elizabeth Anscombe's *Modern Moral Philosophy*
Hannah Arendt's *The Human Condition*
Aristotle's *Metaphysics*
Aristotle's *Nicomachean Ethics*
Edmund Gettier's *Is Justified True Belief Knowledge?*
Georg Wilhelm Friedrich Hegel's *Phenomenology of Spirit*
David Hume's *Dialogues Concerning Natural Religion*
David Hume's *The Enquiry for Human Understanding*
Immanuel Kant's *Religion within the Boundaries of Mere Reason*
Immanuel Kant's *Critique of Pure Reason*
Søren Kierkegaard's *The Sickness Unto Death*
Søren Kierkegaard's *Fear and Trembling*
C. S. Lewis's *The Abolition of Man*
Alasdair MacIntyre's *After Virtue*
Marcus Aurelius's *Meditations*
Friedrich Nietzsche's *On the Genealogy of Morality*
Friedrich Nietzsche's *Beyond Good and Evil*
Plato's *Republic*
Plato's *Symposium*
Jean-Jacques Rousseau's *The Social Contract*
Gilbert Ryle's *The Concept of Mind*
Baruch Spinoza's *Ethics*
Sun Tzu's *The Art of War*
Ludwig Wittgenstein's *Philosophical Investigations*

POLITICS

Benedict Anderson's *Imagined Communities*
Aristotle's *Politics*
Bernard Bailyn's *The Ideological Origins of the American Revolution*
Edmund Burke's *Reflections on the Revolution in France*
John C. Calhoun's *A Disquisition on Government*
Ha-Joon Chang's *Kicking Away the Ladder*
Hamid Dabashi's *Iran: A People Interrupted*
Hamid Dabashi's *Theology of Discontent: The Ideological Foundation of the Islamic Revolution in Iran*
Robert Dahl's *Democracy and its Critics*
Robert Dahl's *Who Governs?*
David Brion Davis's *The Problem of Slavery in the Age of Revolution*

The Macat Library By Discipline

Alexis De Tocqueville's *Democracy in America*
James Ferguson's *The Anti-Politics Machine*
Frank Dikotter's *Mao's Great Famine*
Sheila Fitzpatrick's *Everyday Stalinism*
Eric Foner's *Reconstruction: America's Unfinished Revolution, 1863-1877*
Milton Friedman's *Capitalism and Freedom*
Francis Fukuyama's *The End of History and the Last Man*
John Lewis Gaddis's *We Now Know: Rethinking Cold War History*
Ernest Gellner's *Nations and Nationalism*
David Graeber's *Debt: the First 5000 Years*
Antonio Gramsci's *The Prison Notebooks*
Alexander Hamilton, John Jay & James Madison's *The Federalist Papers*
Friedrich Hayek's *The Road to Serfdom*
Christopher Hill's *The World Turned Upside Down*
Thomas Hobbes's *Leviathan*
John A. Hobson's *Imperialism: A Study*
Samuel P. Huntington's *The Clash of Civilizations and the Remaking of World Order*
Tony Judt's *Postwar: A History of Europe Since 1945*
David C. Kang's *China Rising: Peace, Power and Order in East Asia*
Paul Kennedy's *The Rise and Fall of Great Powers*
Robert Keohane's *After Hegemony*
Martin Luther King Jr.'s *Why We Can't Wait*
Henry Kissinger's *World Order: Reflections on the Character of Nations and the Course of History*
John Locke's *Two Treatises of Government*
Niccolò Machiavelli's *The Prince*
Thomas Robert Malthus's *An Essay on the Principle of Population*
Mahmood Mamdani's *Citizen and Subject: Contemporary Africa And The Legacy Of Late Colonialism*
Karl Marx's *Capital*
John Stuart Mill's *On Liberty*
John Stuart Mill's *Utilitarianism*
Hans Morgenthau's *Politics Among Nations*
Thomas Paine's *Common Sense*
Thomas Paine's *Rights of Man*
Thomas Piketty's *Capital in the Twenty-First Century*
Robert D. Putman's *Bowling Alone*
John Rawls's *Theory of Justice*
Jean-Jacques Rousseau's *The Social Contract*
Theda Skocpol's *States and Social Revolutions*
Adam Smith's *The Wealth of Nations*
Sun Tzu's *The Art of War*
Henry David Thoreau's *Civil Disobedience*
Thucydides's *The History of the Peloponnesian War*
Kenneth Waltz's *Theory of International Politics*
Max Weber's *Politics as a Vocation*
Odd Arne Westad's *The Global Cold War: Third World Interventions And The Making Of Our Times*

POSTCOLONIAL STUDIES

Roland Barthes's *Mythologies*
Frantz Fanon's *Black Skin, White Masks*
Homi K. Bhabha's *The Location of Culture*
Gustavo Gutiérrez's *A Theology of Liberation*
Edward Said's *Orientalism*
Gayatri Chakravorty Spivak's *Can the Subaltern Speak?*

PSYCHOLOGY

Gordon Allport's *The Nature of Prejudice*
Alan Baddeley & Graham Hitch's *Aggression: A Social Learning Analysis*
Albert Bandura's *Aggression: A Social Learning Analysis*
Leon Festinger's *A Theory of Cognitive Dissonance*
Sigmund Freud's *The Interpretation of Dreams*
Betty Friedan's *The Feminine Mystique*
Michael R. Gottfredson & Travis Hirschi's *A General Theory of Crime*
Eric Hoffer's *The True Believer: Thoughts on the Nature of Mass Movements*
William James's *Principles of Psychology*
Elizabeth Loftus's *Eyewitness Testimony*
A. H. Maslow's *A Theory of Human Motivation*
Stanley Milgram's *Obedience to Authority*
Steven Pinker's *The Better Angels of Our Nature*
Oliver Sacks's *The Man Who Mistook His Wife For a Hat*
Richard Thaler & Cass Sunstein's *Nudge: Improving Decisions About Health, Wealth and Happiness*
Amos Tversky's *Judgment under Uncertainty: Heuristics and Biases*
Philip Zimbardo's *The Lucifer Effect*

SCIENCE

Rachel Carson's *Silent Spring*
William Cronon's *Nature's Metropolis: Chicago And The Great West*
Alfred W. Crosby's *The Columbian Exchange*
Charles Darwin's *On the Origin of Species*
Richard Dawkin's *The Selfish Gene*
Thomas Kuhn's *The Structure of Scientific Revolutions*
Geoffrey Parker's *Global Crisis: War, Climate Change and Catastrophe in the Seventeenth Century*
Mathis Wackernagel & William Rees's *Our Ecological Footprint*

SOCIOLOGY

Michelle Alexander's *The New Jim Crow: Mass Incarceration in the Age of Colorblindness*
Gordon Allport's *The Nature of Prejudice*
Albert Bandura's *Aggression: A Social Learning Analysis*
Hanna Batatu's *The Old Social Classes And The Revolutionary Movements Of Iraq*
Ha-Joon Chang's *Kicking Away the Ladder*
W. E. B. Du Bois's *The Souls of Black Folk*
Émile Durkheim's *On Suicide*
Frantz Fanon's *Black Skin, White Masks*
Frantz Fanon's *The Wretched of the Earth*
Eric Foner's *Reconstruction: America's Unfinished Revolution, 1863-1877*
Eugene Genovese's *Roll, Jordan, Roll: The World the Slaves Made*
Jack Goldstone's *Revolution and Rebellion in the Early Modern World*
Antonio Gramsci's *The Prison Notebooks*
Richard Herrnstein & Charles A Murray's *The Bell Curve: Intelligence and Class Structure in American Life*
Eric Hoffer's *The True Believer: Thoughts on the Nature of Mass Movements*
Jane Jacobs's *The Death and Life of Great American Cities*
Robert Lucas's *Why Doesn't Capital Flow from Rich to Poor Countries?*
Jay Macleod's *Ain't No Makin' It: Aspirations and Attainment in a Low Income Neighborhood*
Elaine May's *Homeward Bound: American Families in the Cold War Era*
Douglas McGregor's *The Human Side of Enterprise*
C. Wright Mills's *The Sociological Imagination*

The Macat Library By Discipline

Thomas Piketty's *Capital in the Twenty-First Century*
Robert D. Putman's *Bowling Alone*
David Riesman's *The Lonely Crowd: A Study of the Changing American Character*
Edward Said's *Orientalism*
Joan Wallach Scott's *Gender and the Politics of History*
Theda Skocpol's *States and Social Revolutions*
Max Weber's *The Protestant Ethic and the Spirit of Capitalism*

THEOLOGY

Augustine's *Confessions*
Benedict's *Rule of St Benedict*
Gustavo Gutiérrez's *A Theology of Liberation*
Carole Hillenbrand's *The Crusades: Islamic Perspectives*
David Hume's *Dialogues Concerning Natural Religion*
Immanuel Kant's *Religion within the Boundaries of Mere Reason*
Ernst Kantorowicz's *The King's Two Bodies: A Study in Medieval Political Theology*
Søren Kierkegaard's *The Sickness Unto Death*
C. S. Lewis's *The Abolition of Man*
Saba Mahmood's *The Politics of Piety: The Islamic Revival and the Feminist Subject*
Baruch Spinoza's *Ethics*
Keith Thomas's *Religion and the Decline of Magic*

COMING SOON

Chris Argyris's *The Individual and the Organisation*
Seyla Benhabib's *The Rights of Others*
Walter Benjamin's *The Work Of Art in the Age of Mechanical Reproduction*
John Berger's *Ways of Seeing*
Pierre Bourdieu's *Outline of a Theory of Practice*
Mary Douglas's *Purity and Danger*
Roland Dworkin's *Taking Rights Seriously*
James G. March's *Exploration and Exploitation in Organisational Learning*
Ikujiro Nonaka's *A Dynamic Theory of Organizational Knowledge Creation*
Griselda Pollock's *Vision and Difference*
Amartya Sen's *Inequality Re-Examined*
Susan Sontag's *On Photography*
Yasser Tabbaa's *The Transformation of Islamic Art*
Ludwig von Mises's *Theory of Money and Credit*

The Macat Library By Discipline

Macat Disciplines

Access the greatest ideas and thinkers across entire disciplines, including

Postcolonial Studies

Roland Barthes's *Mythologies*
Frantz Fanon's *Black Skin, White Masks*
Homi K. Bhabha's *The Location of Culture*
Gustavo Gutiérrez's *A Theology of Liberation*
Edward Said's *Orientalism*
Gayatri Chakravorty Spivak's *Can the Subaltern Speak?*

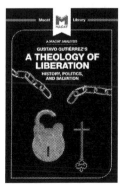

Macat analyses are available from all good bookshops and libraries.

Access hundreds of analyses through one, multimedia tool.
Join free for one month **library.macat.com**

Macat Disciplines

Access the greatest ideas and thinkers across entire disciplines, including

AFRICANA STUDIES

Chinua Achebe's *An Image of Africa:*
Racism in Conrad's Heart of Darkness

W. E. B. Du Bois's *The Souls of Black Folk*

Zora Neale Hurston's *Characteristics of Negro Expression*

Martin Luther King Jr.'s *Why We Can't Wait*

Toni Morrison's *Playing in the Dark:*
Whiteness in the American Literary Imagination

Macat analyses are available from all good bookshops and libraries.

Access hundreds of analyses through one, multimedia tool.

Join free for one month **library.mac .com**

Macat Disciplines

Access the greatest ideas and thinkers across entire disciplines, including

FEMINISM, GENDER AND QUEER STUDIES

Simone De Beauvoir's
The Second Sex

Michel Foucault's
History of Sexuality

Betty Friedan's
The Feminine Mystique

Saba Mahmood's
*The Politics of Piety:
The Islamic Revival and
the Feminist Subject*

Joan Wallach Scott's
*Gender and the
Politics of History*

Mary Wollstonecraft's
*A Vindication of the
Rights of Woman*

Virginia Woolf's
A Room of One's Own

Judith Butler's
Gender Trouble

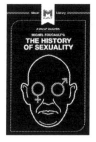

Macat analyses are available from all good bookshops and libraries.

Access hundreds of analyses through one, multimedia tool.
Join free for one month **library.macat.com**

Macat Disciplines

Access the greatest ideas and thinkers across entire disciplines, including

CRIMINOLOGY

Michelle Alexander's
The New Jim Crow: Mass Incarceration in the Age of Colorblindness

Michael R. Gottfredson & Travis Hirschi's
A General Theory of Crime

Elizabeth Loftus's
Eyewitness Testimony

Richard Herrnstein & Charles A. Murray's
The Bell Curve: Intelligence and Class Structure in American Life

Jay Macleod's
Ain't No Makin' It: Aspirations and Attainment in a Low-Income Neighborhood

Philip Zimbardo's
The Lucifer Effect

Macat analyses are available from all good bookshops and libraries.

Access hundreds of analyses through one, multimedia tool.

Join free for one month **library.macat.com**

Macat Disciplines

Access the greatest ideas and thinkers across entire disciplines, including

INEQUALITY

Ha-Joon Chang's, *Kicking Away the Ladder*

David Graeber's, *Debt: The First 5000 Years*

Robert E. Lucas's, *Why Doesn't Capital Flow from Rich To Poor Countries?*

Thomas Piketty's, *Capital in the Twenty-First Century*

Amartya Sen's, *Inequality Re-Examined*

Mahbub Ul Haq's, *Reflections on Human Development*

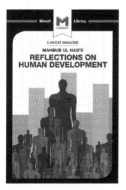

Macat analyses are available from all good bookshops and libraries.

Access hundreds of analyses through one, multimedia tool.
Join free for one month **library.macat.com**

Printed in the United States
by Baker & Taylor Publisher Services